Early Literature of Lacemaking

OLD POINT LACE,
AND HOW TO COPY
AND IMITATE IT
Daisy Waterhouse Hawkins

POINT AND PILLOW LACE
A. Mary Sharp

LACE: ITS ORIGIN
AND HISTORY
Samuel L. Goldenberg

COACHWHIP PUBLICATIONS
Landisville, Pennsylvania

ALSO AVAILABLE:

Ancient and Medieval Dyes
William F. Leggett
ISBN 1-930585-89-6

Early Literature of Lacemaking
Copyright © 2009 Coachwhip Publications

ISBN 1-930585-94-2
ISBN-13 978-1-930585-94-2

Cover: Lace © Brian Chase

CoachwhipBooks.com

All Rights Reserved. No part of this publication may be reproduced, stored in a retrieval system or transmitted in any form or by any means—electronic, mechanical, photocopy, recording or any other—except for brief quotations in printed reviews, without the prior permission of the author or publisher.

Contents

Old Point Lace, and How to Copy and Imitate It

5

Point and Pillow Lace

29

Lace: Its Origin and History

107

Old Point Lace, and How to Copy and Imitate It

Daisy Waterhouse Hawkins

(1878)

Preface

The following facsimiles of Point-Lace are selected from specimens in the valuable collection at the South Kensington Museum, and are published with the sanction of the authorities of that Institution, for which sanction the Author is very grateful, as she is thus afforded an opportunity of diffusing among the public a few antique examples, as standard models of beauty to those who now endeavour to revive the long-neglected art of needle lace-making.

D. W. H.

Old Point Lace

The object of the present work is to assist in remedying a great defect of most modern amateur lace, viz., a mistaken style of pattern. The aim of making lace by hand is to revive the ancient art, of which such beautiful specimens have survived the decay of centuries. So far as the materials employed, and the delicacy and variety of stitches, the same degree of perfection has been already attained by many of our modern workers as by their ancient predecessors. But in spite of the care and industry bestowed, and the great strain on patience and eyesight involved, there is still one most important portion of the work which continues to be comparatively neglected, and that is, *the design*, in consequence of which neglect, modern point lace is, when compared with old lace, like a body without a soul.

This want of variety and beauty in design is the more remarkable, since the work is chiefly undertaken by the most refined enjoyers of "elegant leisure," who are supposed to possess an amount of delicate fancy and taste, scarcely to be expected from those who "stitch, stitch, stitch," merely to keep themselves alive on bread and tea.

The difference between the patterns now used for point lace and the old specimens is this,—the modern lace consists of an exact and continuous repetition of a design, which is contained in four or five inches of space, whereas the old lace displays a constant variety and change in the pattern throughout the entire length of the piece; there is also a freedom and originality in the design which constitutes its chief beauty. In this consists the superiority of *hand* over *machine* made lace. The iron machinery can repeat network stitches by the million, with greater precision and rapidity than any fair fingers can attain, but at best such repetition is tedious to the eye.

The charm of variety and the beauty of novelty can only be found in the work of skilled hands, guided by fanciful minds, and not in the productions of iron wheels set a-going by steam.

In order to a complete restoration of the art of point lace making, each worker should design and amplify the pattern as the work progresses; but this would require an amount of invention not possessed by many, and to those who have it not, the following pages will be useful. In them are shown exact copies of admirable pieces of old lace preserved in the South Kensington Museum; each one is of a different style or period, and is a good specimen of its class. To facilitate the reproduction of this old lace, a diagram for working accompanies each specimen, and in this diagram the design is so modified as to render it easy by the present abbreviated method of working.

In the old lace may be remarked an absence of geometrical precision, and in the most ancient, a certain uncouthness which has a charm of its own, and which contrasts very favourably with many of the patterns of the present day, in which geometrical stiffness and monotonous similarity are the most remarkable features.

It is hoped that this book, by aiding some fair votaries of point lace to really *copy* the beautiful old relics of antique art-work(wo)-manship, may induce them to aim still higher, so that by exerting the fanciful and imaginative faculties so largely possessed by the refined of the fair sex, they may attain the same perfection in diversity and beauty of design, that they have already achieved in the more mechanical portion of their art.

How to Copy and Imitate Old Point Lace

In order to render the present volume useful to those who are novices in the art of lace-making, as well as to those who are already proficient, it is necessary not only to make a display of beautiful designs, but also to describe the means by which the same designs can be reproduced with needle and thread.

Having procured the necessary materials, viz., linen thread, linen lace braid, cord, and good needles, select a braid of the width indicated by the pattern, and tack it firmly on to the pattern between the parallel lines. Where a fulness is caused at either edge of the braid by the curves, whip over the edge of the braid, and thus draw it to the shape. Where two braids come in contact, sew them finely but firmly together by the outer threads.

All the varied stitches with which the scrolls are filled, and all the bars or "brides" are produced by button-hole-stitch, worked (as in embroidery) *from left to right*, and each row below the other. Bearing this rule in mind, it is easy for every worker to originate fresh varieties of stitches during the progress of her work.

Venetian or Spanish Rose Point is to be copied without the introduction of any braid. A series of threads (or if preferred a fine cord) should be tacked on to the pattern, following the exact outline of every scroll, and afterwards sewn over, the intervening space being filled entirely with button-hole-stitch. Attach a needleful of thread firmly to the outline threads or cord at the right-hand side, carry it tightly across the space to the left-hand side and attach it there, then work a row of button-hole-stitch very small and even, taking each stitch through the outline of the scroll, and

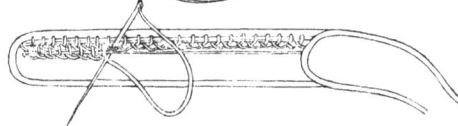

Fig. 1

including in it the thread that is fastened across. Continue to work other rows in the same manner until the scroll is filled up. Observe that these rows of stitches generally run in a horizontal direction with regard to the whole piece of lace, as though the work had been executed as far as possible whilst retaining it in its ultimate intended position towards the beholder.

Another method of rendering this filling-in stitch still more close and perfect is to be seen in Fig. 2. After fastening the thread across, and working the first row of close button-hole-stitch over it, form the second and subsequent rows by taking each stitch through the close threads of each stitch in the row above, instead of through the loops between the stitches. This causes the stitches to be more square and firm, but in very fine work

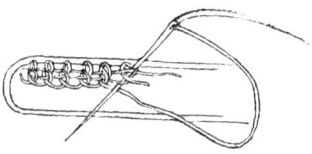

Fig. 2

it adds considerably to the time and care occupied. It will of course be understood that in all these diagrams the stitches are greatly magnified and separated in order to make the working intelligible. After practicing the foregoing stitches, fig. 3 will easily be understood without further explanation, and after working that, the fair lace-maker will perceive that by increasing the number of stitches to four or five and shortening the loops, a chessboard pattern is produced; and that by shortening the stitches and lengthening the loops, a dotted network is made. Another variety is

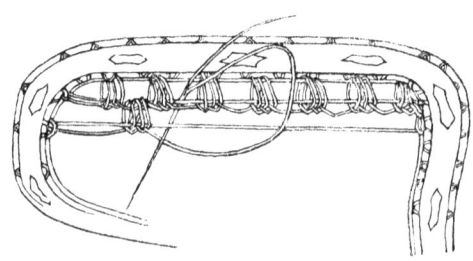

Fig. 3

shown in fig. 4. Work a loose button-hole-stitch all round the interior of the scroll; for second and subsequent rows, take each stitch through the loop above, and then knot it, by passing the needle a second time through the same loop, and drawing it tight before commencing another stitch. This construction may again be changed, by working the second row and knots

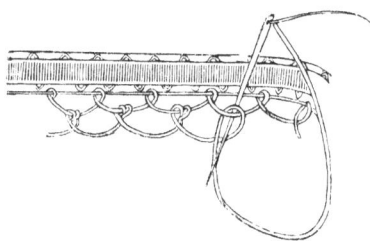

Fig. 4

between the two threads of the button-hole-stitch, as shown in fig. 5; but for this square network it is necessary to make the loops much longer than in any of the stitches previously described. Bars or "brides" are made by working very tight button-hole-stitches round one thread (or more) that has been fastened across from one scroll to another. If bars are required broad and flat, fasten two, or more, threads across, and then darn them together instead of button-hold stitching.

Having now described all the deviations of stitch necessary in carrying out the lace designs in the present volume, it is hoped that every worker will add to their beauty and originality by introducing additional varieties of her own fancy.

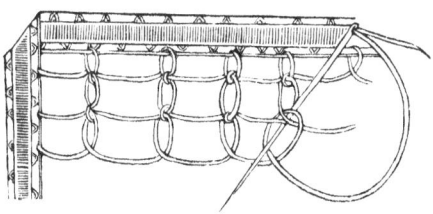

Fig. 5

Flemish Lace Without Brides (N° 586)

Pattern for Copying Flemish Lace (N° 586) With Braid and Stitches

Flemish Lace (N° 596)

Pattern for Copying Flemish Lace With Braid Bride and Stitches

Lace With Plain Brides (N° 1586)

Pattern for Copying Flemish Lace (Nº 1586) With Braid Brides and Stitches

Flemish Lace Edging (Nº 586)

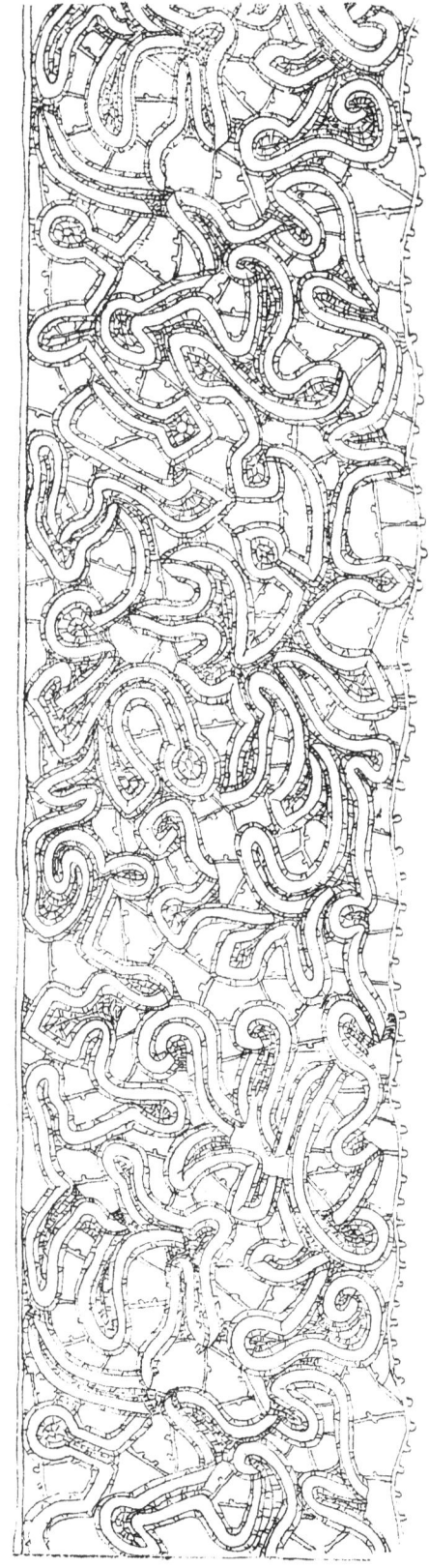

Pattern for Copying Lace Edging (N° 586) With Tight Braid & Brides Only

Italian Lace Edging (Nº 583)

Pattern for Copying Italian Lace (N° 583) With Braid Cord Brides & Stitches

Italian Rose Point

Pattern for Copying Italian Rose Point, With Needle & Thread

Narrow Lace in the Book Collection

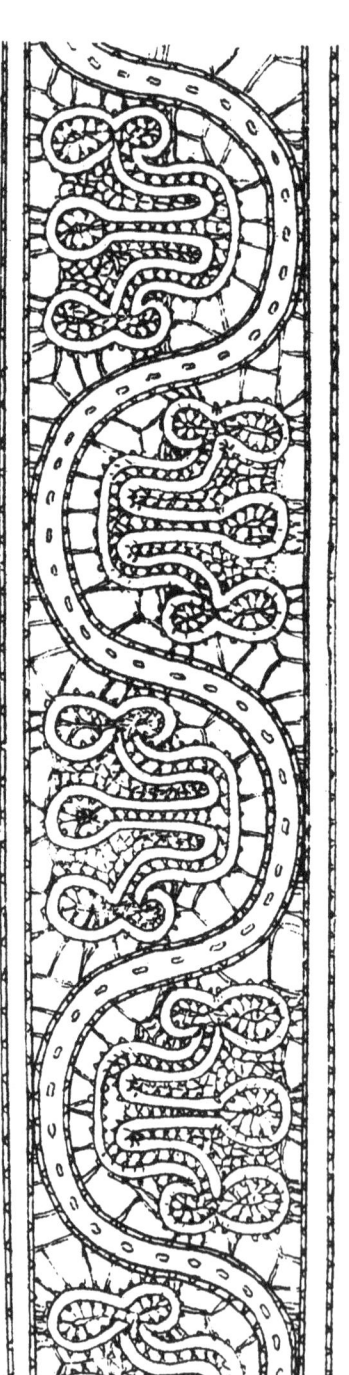

Pattern for Imitating Narrow Lace Plate 13

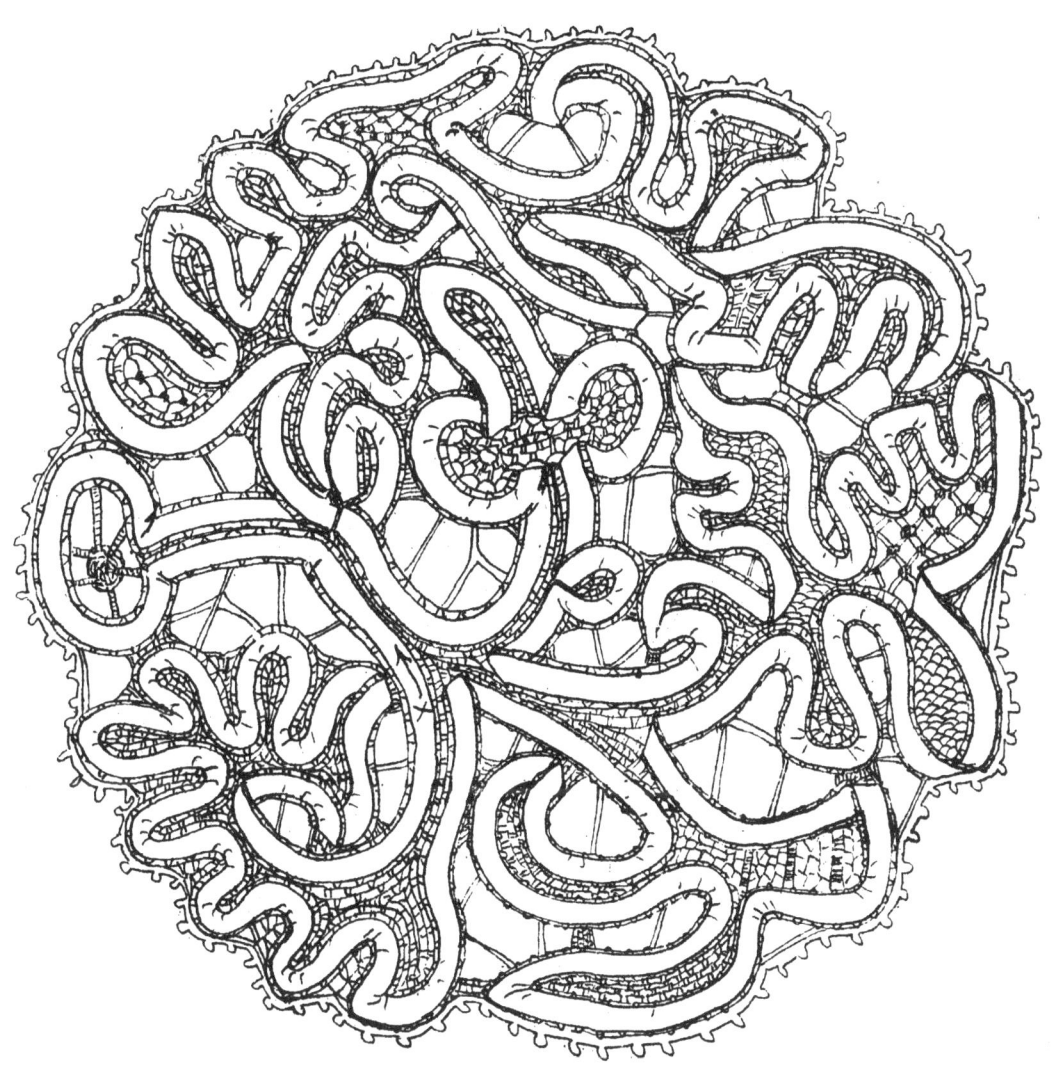

Original Design for Working Lace D'Oyley,
With Braid Brides and Stitches

A Curious Piece of Italian Lace (N° 582) in Which Pieces of Tape are Introduced

Old Point Lace

Curious Specimen of Portuguese Lace (N° 584) in Which Two Different Patterns are Joined

Portrait of the
Princess Eleonora of Mantua

Point and Pillow Lace

A. Mary Sharp

(1899)

Preface

The object of this little book is to supply to owners and lovers of Lace some clear information easily referred to, by means of which they can ascertain the true name and nature of any particular specimen.

The valuable works of which a list is given on page xiii, as the authorities consulted, are some of them, especially the late Mrs. Palliser's *History of Lace*, almost exhaustive as to the historical records on the subject, and they also contain a great deal of interesting information concerning the various lace manufactures. Yet the writer has found, in common she believes with others, that a diligent search through many volumes and much inquiry of experts has been necessary before some particular piece of Lace could be identified, even if in the end that identification did not appear doubtful.

In the present volume it is hoped that the simple statements distinguishing the features of each variety will enable the reader to recognise them readily, especially as each description is accompanied by an illustration, on as large a scale as the size of the page will allow, so that the texture of the Lace may be the more easily seen.

That description alone, however good, without illustrations is very insufficient will readily be allowed by anyone who attempts the task of explaining in words the nature and peculiarities of any kind of Lace. Dr. Johnson gives as a definition of "net," "a texture woven with intersticial vacuities," and of "network," "anything reticulated or decussated, at equal distances, with interstices between the intersections." Where the great lexicographer failed to make his meaning more intelligible to simple folk, lesser mortals may well be glad to eke out their otherwise insufficient explanations by the help of the photographer.

One difficulty attendant on the study of Lace must be mentioned. It is that at various times the same kinds of Lace were made in different localities, each imitating the other. Thus Brussels and Alençon copied Venice, and Italy in turn adopted the "réseau" ground in imitation of Flanders; nor is the reason far to seek. The laws of supply and demand were in force three hundred years ago as now, and though we are apt to think of the countries of Europe, before the days of railways and steamboats, as isolated, yet a very cursory study of history is enough to prove that it was far otherwise. The number of travellers was no doubt much less than at present, but the richer classes were socially in constant communication with each other everywhere, as is indeed evidenced by the prevalence of the same fashions in dress throughout Europe at any given time. No sooner did the ladies of Paris in the time of Henry the Fourth adopt the high ruff, than English ladies hastened to do the same; and as soon as the Pillow laces of Genoa were admired and found suitable to the falling collars of the succeeding reigns, the lace-workers of Flanders were quick in learning to reproduce the style, in this case so exactly, that but little difference can now be detected between their work and that of the Italians. Lace also was largely made in convents and lace-making was taught in convent schools; and the fact that nuns were of all nationalities helps to account for the cosmopolitan character of the Art.

It will not be attempted here to decide from what locality any particular Lace may have come, but merely to state on good authority to what style it belongs, and to assist the reader, by a careful description of its details, to judge for himself or herself of its character. Of all the decorative works of Art Lace is by far the most perishable; indeed, it may be said that the more beautiful the Lace, the more delicate and more easily destroyed it is.

Much has disappeared long ago, and in the hands of ignorant owners the little that has lasted till now is in danger of being finally lost. If, therefore, what is here written should attract the notice of some who have taken but small care of their frail possessions, and have, without scruple, given them over to the tender mercies of the dressmaker who cuts, or the washerwoman who tears, and if they should be induced henceforth to pay more heed to these irreplaceable treasures, the writer will feel that she has not written in vain on a subject which has long been one of great interest to herself.

She cannot send this little book into the world without expressing her thanks to Mr. Alan Cole, of the Science and Art Department, South Kensington, for the help and advice that he has been good enough to give her on a subject on which he is so well-known an authority; also to the kind friends to whom she is indebted for the loan of many beautiful specimens of lace here represented. Without such assistance and encouragement her pleasant task might never have been accomplished at all.

A. M. S.
Ufton Court, July, 1899.

A Glossary of Terms Used

Point lace.—From the French "point," a stitch—properly applied only to Lace made with needle stitches, or Needle-point lace. This term has been often much misapplied. Neither "Point d'Angleterre," nor "Punto di Milano," nor "Honiton Point" are Point laces at all in the proper sense of the words; they are Pillow lace.

Pillow lace, or Bone lace, or Dentelle au fuseau, or Merletti a Piombini, is Lace made on the pillow with bobbins; hence the English, French and Italian names, the bobbins being sometimes made of bone or lead as well as of wood.

Toilé.—The substance of the pattern as contrasted with the groundwork.

Réseau.—The network ground in which the pattern is sometimes set.

Brides.—The slender stalks or ties connecting different parts of the pattern together when not on a net ground.

Picots.—The knots or thorns which often decorate "brides" and also the edges of the pattern.

À jours.—The open ornamental work introduced in enclosed spaces.

Cordonnet.—The thick thread or cord with which the pattern is often outlined.

Appliqué denotes when the pattern, either Needlework or Pillow, is made separately and afterwards sewn on to a net ground.

Guipure.—The cord or gimp sometimes overcast with stitches; frequently used for outlining heavy Laces. "Guiper" is an old verb, meaning to roll round a cord. The term "Guipure" has often been wrongly applied to various kinds of Lace. It is here used to denote only Lace of which the pattern consists of a cord or tape connected by "brides."

Authorities Consulted

Alan Cole, *Ancient Needle-point and Pillow Lace*.
Brazza, *A Guide to Old and New Lace in Italy*.
Catalogue of South Kensington Museum.
Madame Despierres, *Histoire du Point d'Alençon*.
Doumert, *La Dentelle*.
Felkin, *Machine-wrought Lace*.
Lefebure, *Embroidery and Lace*.
Mrs. Palliser, *History of Lace*.
Seguin, *La Dentelle*.
Mrs. Treadwin, *Antique Point and Honiton*,
The "Queen" Lace Book.
Urbani Gheltof, *Trattato Storico*.

Of Lace in General

The English word Lace is taken from the French "Lacis," a term however, which, when properly used, denotes only the Italian work "Punto a maglia," or Darned netting.

There are two distinct kinds of Hand-made lace; first, Lace made with the needle, that is, Needle-point lace, under which heading the above-mentioned Darned netting may be included, and secondly, Lace made on a pillow with bobbins, that is, Pillow lace.

Machine-made lace will be treated of in a separate section later on, and is not now therefore taken into account.

In order to distinguish between Needle-point and Pillow lace, and to decide to which of the two classes any particular specimen belongs, both the "toilé" or solid part of the pattern and also the grounding, whether of "brides" or of network, should be closely examined.

In Needle-point lace the solid parts are always made of rows of looped, or so-called button-hole stitches, sometimes quite closely worked, as in the specimen given in Fig. 1, Illustration I., sometimes looser or with small open spaces left in patterns; still the stitch used is always the same.

The "brides" in Needle-point consist of one or two threads fastened across from one part of the pattern to another and then closely whipped or button-holed over; they are usually more or less decorated with "picots," made much in the same manner as the "bride" itself. (See Fig. 5, Illustration I.)

But Needle-point is also sometimes grounded with "réseau" or network, and still this when examined will be found to be made with the same stitch. The meshes of the network are merely loose looped stitches; sometimes the needle is twisted a second time in each stitch to keep the mesh open, as in Fig. 2, Illustration I.; sometimes the work is strengthened with a second thread, which is whipped over all along the row at the base of the meshes, as in Fig. 3, Illustration I.

Thus it will be seen that though other stitches were employed in the earlier linen lace-work, such as Drawn-work, Cut-work and Reticella (see Fig, 5, Illustration I.), yet for true Needle-point lace, with all its beautiful varieties of design and ornament, one stitch alone sufficed, namely, what we have called the looped or button-hole stitch, in Italian "Punto a festone."

Pillow lace, when carefully examined, will be found to be constructed in a fundamentally different manner. The "toilé" will in every case be seen to be composed of threads

Illustration I.
Details of Needle-Point Lace, Magnified

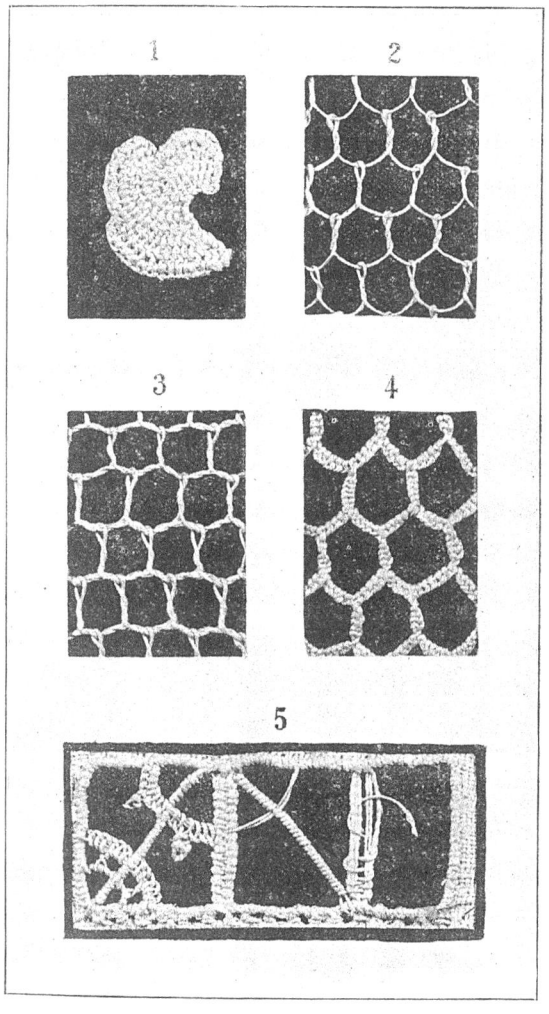

1. Toilé of Needle-point. 2. Réseau of Brussels Point.
3. Réseau of Alençon Point. 4. Réseau of Argentan Point.
5. Unfinished specimen of Cut-work or Reticella.

crossing each other more or less at right angles, and in and out like the texture of cambric or other woven cloth. This is shown in Fig. 1, Illustration II.

The "brides," when made on the pillow, consist of twisted or plaited threads, and the "picots" of simple loops; it should, however, be remarked that "brides" worked with the needle are often added to Pillow-made lace, which is then called "Mixed lace," and in that case they will be seen to be made of button-hole stitch as above described.

The "réseau" work of Pillow lace is much more varied than that of Needle-point; the specimens given in Illustration II. by no means exhaust all the varieties, though the peculiar "réseaux" of the best-known Laces are there given. They will be described in connection with each kind later on. It is sufficient here to say that in all Pillow lace the network is made by twisting and plaiting the threads, sometimes in twos and sometimes in fours, as the case may be. Thus, roughly speaking, the broad difference between Point and Pillow lace is that the first is worked throughout with looped stitches, and the second is made with twisted or plaited threads, which last is in fact weaving, though the work is done with the hands and bobbins and not with the loom. Theoretically the difference as here stated is very simple, yet it must be allowed that practically in the case of very fine Lace it is not always at first sight easy of detection, and for a beginner at all events it may be often difficult to recognise the above-described details except with the aid of a magnifying glass; when once these are seen, however, it should be easy for anyone to make the distinction between Pillow and Needle-point lace, and also, following the further descriptions given later on, to identify any special specimen. What has been said above does not apply to Darned netting, which, being usually coarse, does not require special description here.

Having been able, with some confidence, to identify any particular specimen, whether it is Point or Pillow lace, or Venetian, French or Flemish in style, the further question is often asked, "How old do you think that piece of Lace is?"

There are several indications that will help to answer that inquiry. We know of certain styles of Lace that they were invented at a certain time, and that they were worn during certain periods, and in this connection contemporary portrait art is of great service and interest. Moreover, it is generally found to be the case that the style of design at each centre of the lace-making art went through a definite and very easily traced course of development. The Lace made at Alençon or Mechlin during the seventeenth century, for instance, was very noticeably different in the style of the patterns from what was produced in the eighteenth century, and it was the same elsewhere. In fact the same laws seem to have governed Art in every direction, and as Architecture passed through various styles which can be recognised and apportioned to different periods, so also in its degree did the Art of lace-making.

In the illustrations given further on the carefully selected representative collection of the various styles will, it is hoped, be found useful in assisting the student to classify any Lace that may come under notice.

Yet the matter, it must be confessed, is somewhat complicated by the fact that some styles of Lace continued to be produced during long periods of time, even after later fashions were developed. Cut-work in particular was made with very little, if any, change in the style of design during two or even three centuries; and in the case of the simpler kinds of Pillow lace, the parchment patterns on which it was made were often treasured and handed down from one generation of lace-workers to another; one family, from mother to daughter, confining themselves to working a few patterns only, which they naturally continued to make as long as there was a demand for them. This is the case at the present

Illustration II.
Details of Pillow-Lace, Magnified

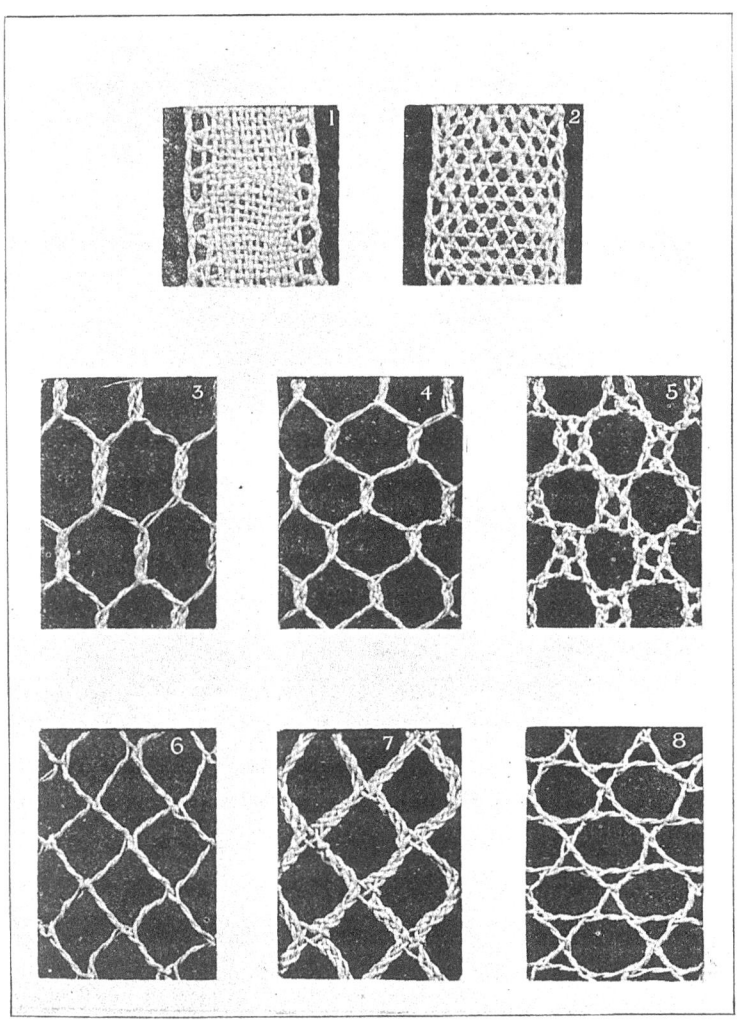

1. Toilé of Pillow-lace.
2. Open Toilé of Brussels Pillow-lace.
3. Réseau of Brussels Pillow-lace.
4. Réseau of Mechlin.
5. Réseau, called "Cinq Trous."
6. Réseau of Lille.
7. Réseau of Valenciennes.
8. Réseau, called "Fond Chant" or "Point de Paris."

day with the manufacture of modern Valenciennes at Ypres and in the neighbourhood. But with these exceptions a study of the construction and style of design of any particular piece of Lace should afford a fair indication of the date of its production.

No indication has been left us to show that what we now call Lace was known at all in Greek and Roman times, and it is rather curious that the fable of Arachne turned into a spider because she rivalled Athene in the delicacy of her needlecraft should have been invented, when no such work as could be said to approach to the fineness of a spider's web was practised till so many centuries later.

Lace, as we now understand it, belongs, like music, essentially to modern times; and taking into account its extreme fragility, it may be said that probably no Lace now existing is older than three hundred years, and that but little of such fine or open Lace as can be used for articles of dress is more than two hundred years old.

The earliest supposed record existing of its practice is in a picture by Quintin Matsys in the church of St. Peter Louvain (date 1495), in which a girl is represented working at a lace-pillow, though it is not possible to identify the kind of Lace upon which she is engaged. Until the middle of the sixteenth century, that is before the reign of Queen Elizabeth, in England at all events, Lace as applied to dress does not appear at all in the portraits of the day. The ladies of Henry the Eighth's court, painted by Holbein, wore plain linen head-dresses and un-trimmed frills at the neck and wrists.

It is interesting in our National Portrait Gallery to be able to see almost the exact time of the introduction of this beautiful Art. Queen Mary Tudor, as there represented, though handsomely dressed, wears linen cuffs embroidered but bare of Lace, not yet then in use, but in the picture next to her in date, already a little lace edging appears round the ruff, and in the portraits of Elizabeth and her courtiers ruffs and Lace together have grown rampant.

And if we cannot attribute a very early date for the invention of the Art of lace-making, neither was it in its perfection of long duration; it suffered much from the rage for simplicity born of the doctrines of J. J. Rousseau in the eighteenth century, and was practically extinguished by the troubles of the French Revolution and by the classical fashions in dress which succeeded them under the Empire.

In France the manufacture of rich Needle lace has to some extent recovered itself. Within the last fifteen or twenty years also great efforts have been made to revive the Art in Venice, and schools have been established in the island of Burano in the neighbourhood. In Belgium neither needle nor pillow lace-making were ever, even in war time, altogether discontinued, but the character of the Lace has been essentially altered. Owing also to the increased cost of labour, such modern Lace naturally commands very high prices, and nowadays when the genius of the inventor has so marvellously perfected the achievements of steam machinery in lace-making, and when such Lace can be bought at astonishingly low prices, it is scarcely to be expected that any real or considerable revival of the Art should take place. All the more, since the exquisite work of former ages is thus practically irreplaceable, must we value such of it as has been preserved to us, with the interest of antiquarians, as well as on account of its intrinsic beauty.

The chief centres of Needle lace-making were Venice, Brussels and Alençon. Of Spanish-point, so called, some may have been made in Spain, most however that goes by that name was certainly Venetian. The Greek Lace, which is a Cut-work of geometrical design, though it has often been bought in the Ionian Islands, was also probably Italian.

Pillow laces of some sort were, at some time or another, made all over Europe, but nowhere else did they attain to such beauty as in Flanders, where, according to some, the Art was invented.

Of Italian laces there are both Needle-point and Pillow. The former take the precedence in date and also in point of beauty; the latter came chiefly from Genoa and the districts in North Italy, as also the varieties of knotted and plaited Laces to be described later on.

Of Italian Needle Lace

Reticella.

In point of design Italian Lace may be classed under four styles: the Mediaeval, the Geometrical, the Renaissance, and the Rococo. Such as belongs to the two first was for the most part worked out of linen and often combined with embroidery. The material spun with the old-world distaff, as still to be seen in the country districts in Italy, and woven under no great pressure of haste on hand-looms in the convent or the cottage, was far superior to anything that can be now procured in purity and strength. It was unmixed with cotton, that cheaper substance which so detracts from the durability and quality of our modern linen manufactures. The specimens of church and household linen preserved to the present day bear sufficient testimony to the good workmanship of the weaver and the excellence of his materials.

The Lace included under the above-mentioned two earlier styles, namely, the Mediaeval and the Geometrical, are Drawn-work, Cut-work, Reticella or so-called Greek Lace, and Lacis or Darned netting. They were produced chiefly during the sixteenth century.

The third or Renaissance style expressed itself in flowing patterns of scroll work, and in a conventional treatment of flowers and other objects. The Lace was worked entirely without a linen foundation. Of this description are all the most beautiful achievements of the Art in Italy during the seventeenth century, namely, the splendid Venetian and so-called Spanish-points.

Lastly came the Rococo style, when boldness and beauty of design were sacrificed to complexity of detail, and when natural objects, and especially flowers, were represented with small regard to symmetry or unity of composition, but often also with marvellous skill and fidelity. The Lace produced during the early part of the eighteenth century in this style, in spite of an overflowing redundancy of ornament, must still challenge admiration by the beauty and ingenuity of the execution; but these merits rapidly disappeared,

Illustration III.

Mediaeval Drawn-work or Punto Tirato.

and the Rococo Lace of a later period became coarse and inferior in workmanship, while the patterns dwindled to stiff and disconnected ornaments, sparsely set in a "réseau" ground.

After this general account of the styles, as they succeeded each other, the laces themselves may be separately described.

Punto Tirato
(*Eng.* Drawn-work.)

This Lace is one of the earliest in point of date, and may be said to be the origin out of which all future lace-work grew. It is made entirely out of a loose linen material, the threads of which are not cut or pulled out, but merely drawn apart from each other and closely sewn over, either with silk or linen thread, thus having the appearance of a network of small square meshes, which forms the ground of the pattern left in the plain linen. The design thus grounded was of necessity angular, but occasionally this angularity is corrected by means of a silk or linen thread embroidered like a "cordonnet" along the outline on the surface of the work. The whole is usually in the form of bands, four or five inches wide, edged with a border of the linen embroidered. The subjects of the designs are often extremely quaint—horses, dogs, birds, besides mythical animals, were

Illustration IV.

Darned Netting, or Punto Ricamato a maglia quadra.

most ambitiously attempted, as is shown in Illustration III. The frequency with which representations especially of horses occur reminds one that they are to this day the favourite subject of popular Art in Venice, where the real animal can never be seen, and suggests a Venetian origin to these designs. But work of the kind was also extensively produced in Spain, and here the designs chosen were usually Oriental in character, heavy scrolls and arabesques suggesting the influence of Moorish taste. In the Greek islands also this work seems to have been made, and in this case with strictly classical patterns, survivals, no doubt, of early Byzantine traditions. Much the same effect was accomplished by means of another kind of early Needle-work lace named—

Punto Ricamato a Maglia Quadra
(*Fr.* Lacis, *Eng.* Darned netting.)

But in this work the ground is supplied by a netting of either silk or linen thread, made with knots in the usual way or sometimes with threads only twisted. The pattern is worked on the netting with a stitch like darning, and also as a variety with an in-and-out stitch like weaving. It appears to have been much in use for church work for sacred emblems, as the lamb and the pelican are often met with, as well as dragons and terrible imaginary beasts of all sorts. (See Illustration IV.) The work remained long in favour, and in later times really beautiful scroll-like patterns in the Renaissance style were so executed. In the South Kensington Museum Collection there are several very gracefully designed borders to silk table-covers in this work, made both of white and coloured threads and of silk of various shades. It is, indeed, surprising to see what an extremely good effect is thus produced by very simple means, and it is to be regretted that when this work was revived a little while ago under the rather inappropriate name of "Guipure d'Art," such very poor patterns should have been preferred to those of the beautiful Italian work of the kind in existence. This work has a special interest, because it introduced into the Art of lace-making the principle of the looped stitch, which is the common foundation of all netting and also of all Needle-point lace-work.

PUNTO TAGLIATO
(*Fr.* Point-coupé, *Eng.* Cut-work)

is an advance on Drawn-work. It is made by cutting squares or rectangular spaces out of the linen and filling them with needle stitches worked on transverse threads. In this work the patterns are geometrical, but they are varied by the rich embroidery generally worked on such plain spaces of the linen as were left. The peculiar character of this embroidery should be noticed, as shown in Illustration V.; the threads composing it are always laid parallel to either the woof or warp of the linen foundation, they are never, as in modern satin stitch, worked diagonally, nor is any padding ever used underneath the embroidery to raise it.

The construction of this kind of Needle lace will be easily seen in the unfinished specimen given in Illustration I., Fig. 5. It will be found to consist of three different stitches, a looped button-hole stitch, a close-sewn rope stitch covering one or two threads, and an in-and-out stitch over two or four threads, called in Italian "Punto di Genoa." These stitches are used in Lace worked out of linen, such as Cut-work and Reticella, and should be carefully noticed and understood if the beautiful work so called is to be properly appreciated. Cut-work, as well as Reticella, is often misnamed Greek Lace.

RETICELLA, OR GREEK LACE

This Lace differs from Cut-work in that though it also is worked out of a linen foundation, the linen has almost entirely disappeared; a narrow, double hemstitched edge at the top and bottom of the band of Lace is all that is discoverable. The threads left as the framework of the pattern, dividing it into square spaces, are covered closely with stitches, and the rest of the material is altogether cut away. Into these squares are introduced diagonal lines and circles arid half circles forming very beautiful and intricate combinations, and enriched with patterns in solid needlework edged with "picots." This Lace is frequently called "Greek Lace," principally owing to the fact that during the English occupation of

Illustration V.

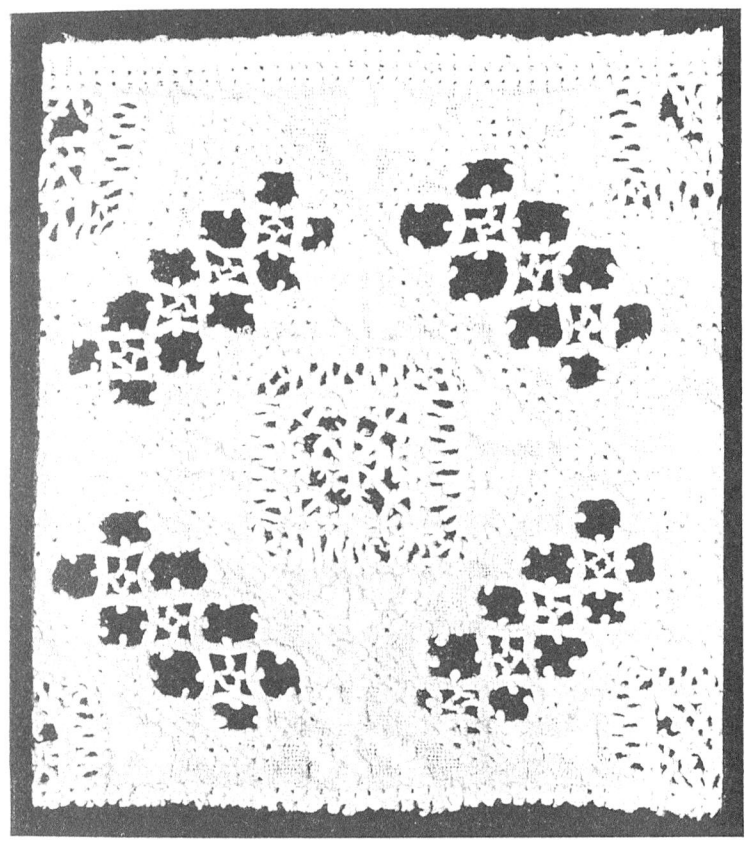

Cut-work, or Punto tagliata.

the Ionian Islands a great deal of it was found there and bought by English visitors. There seems little doubt that it was both made and largely used in Corfu and the neighbouring islands, but it is nevertheless undoubtedly Italian and not Greek in its style and origin. It must be remembered that during the time of its production these Greek islands were in the possession of the Venetian Republic, colonized by Venetians and in constant communication with the mother city; it is not therefore surprising that this Italian Lace should have been imported, imitated and have become naturalised there. At any rate there is no distinctive character either of pattern or execution by which the Lace, even though bought in the Ionian Islands, can be distinguished from Italian Reticella.

The Needlework laces of different kinds described in this chapter, though in use during the fifteenth and the early part of the sixteenth century, were not employed for decoration of dress. It is true that of Lace so used mention is found in records dating as far back as the coronation of Richard the Third, but such Lace seems to have been of silk or of gold or silver, and would be what we should now call braid. It may be remarked that the word

Illustration VI.

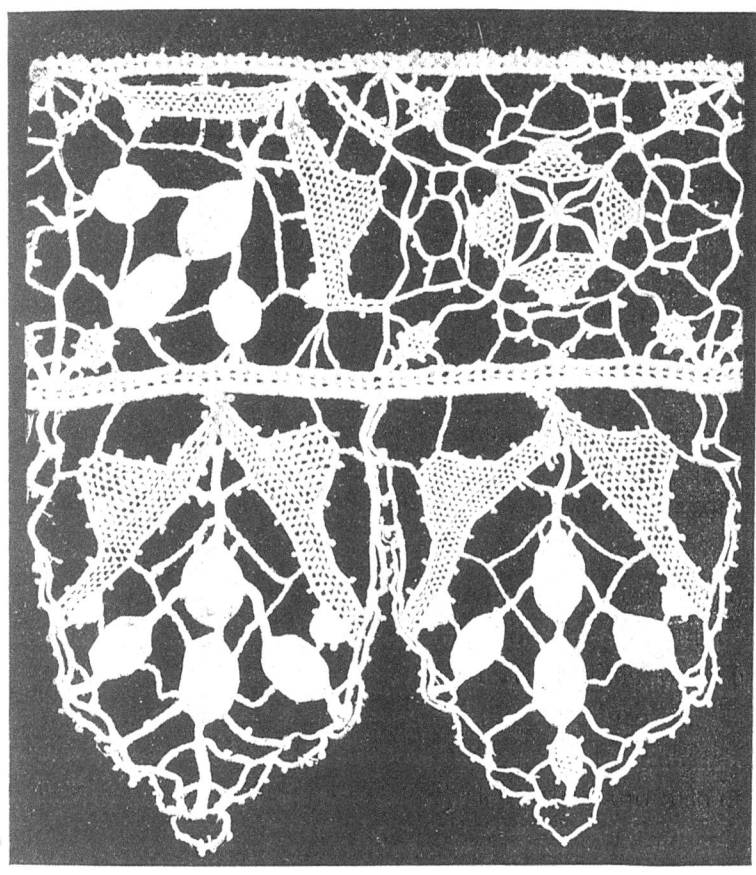

Reticella with Punto in Aria border.

Lace has survived to the present day in this sense, the gold and silver braid now used for uniforms being still so called.

Cut-work and other linen Laces were used to decorate church and household linen of every kind. During the long leisure of convent life skilful hands were continually employed in providing for the adornment of church furniture with needlework both of silk and linen thread, and almost universally in well-to-do households the ladies of the family took pride in seeing that their household linen was ornamented in the same manner. Table-cloths, sheets, pillow-cases and towels made usually of home-spun linen were worked with borders of this kind, a practice which, as is well known, has continued, especially on the Continent, till within the present century. All this, however, now belongs to the past; the Lace has been bought up by the ubiquitous modern tourist after having been cut off in strips, for sale, from the linen out of which it was made, and but little of it now remains in its original condition to explain the purpose for which it was worked. Yet the linen-made Laces of Reticella and Cut-work are singularly well suited for the decoration of table and especially of church linen, and it is surprising that among all the many modern sorts of fancy-work these have not found more frequent imitators. The stitches are, as has been said, very simple, and the work is not too fine for ordinarily good eyesight. The Lace when completed is so good and rich in effect, and so strong for wear, that it can but be wished that fashion will some day inspire industrious and neat-fingered English needlewomen to emulate the beautiful performances of Italian ladies of the sixteenth century.

Of Italian Needle Lace (*Continued.*)

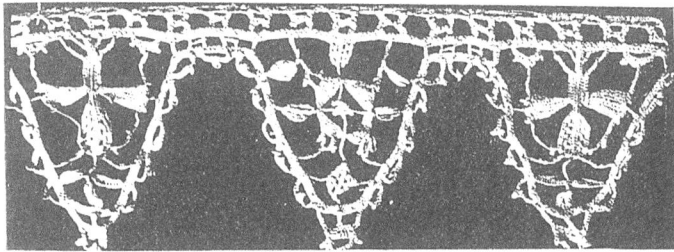

Punto in Aria.

A time came when the restraints imposed on design by the linen foundation were found to be irksome, and it occurred to some innovator to dispense with it altogether and to construct the pattern on threads fastened on parchment in any form that fancy might dictate. This was the beginning of "Punto in Aria," literally "stitches in the air"; that is, without any foundation of linen; and it was by development of this principle that all the subsequent beautiful Needle-points of Italy were made.

At first geometrical forms, which had been of necessity in Cut-work, were still adhered to, though a greater variety of ornament was found possible. Then a pointed edge was worked on threads laid down in the required shape, and the spaces were filled in with patterns of solid or open-work loop stitching executed in an excellent manner, and "brides picotées" were added to connect and strengthen the parts.

A specimen is shown in Illustration VI. of two squares of Reticella with "Punto in Aria" vandykes attached. The Reticella will be seen to be bordered by a narrow double line of hemstitch, showing that it is worked out of a piece of linen; but the vandyke is independent of such foundation. The open Medicis ruff and the cuffs worn by the little Princess of Mantua, as seen in the frontispiece, are of the same kind, namely, a band of Reticella edged with the "Punto in Aria" vandykes. The date of the picture is about 1600.

This introduction of "Punto in Aria" marks a very considerable development in the uses to which Lace was applied. No sooner did this new style of Lace appear, as we may judge from the portraits of the day, than it seems to have taken the world of fashion by storm. Plain linen collars and headdresses were relegated to widows and waiting-maids, and Reticella, hitherto only found serviceable for coarse table-linen, was, in combination with the new edging, and worked in fine lawn, lavished upon cuffs and aprons and the

Raised Venetian Point, or Punto tagliato a foliami.

ruffs that grew to the preposterous dimensions with which we are familiar in the pictures of Queen Elizabeth and her courtiers. These were worn both round and also of the open shape shown in the frontispiece; both shapes seem to have been in fashion together, judging by the well-known picture by Marc Gerrardo representing the state progress of the Queen on her way to pay a visit to Lord Hunsdon, and in which she is surrounded by the ladies and gentlemen of her court, the former wearing some one shaped ruff and some another. This picture was engraved by Vertue, and is of great interest as a record of the costumes of the time.

Of Queen Elizabeth's ruffs much mention is made in the lists of new year's gifts that she was in the habit of receiving from her courtiers. Besides gold and jewellery from the gentlemen, and embroideries, silks, and gifts of all sorts from the ladies, these latter presented her yearly with "ruffes with rabatines of lawne cut-work" and sets of cuffs, both made and unmade; sometimes the "lawne cut-work" was set with seed pearls, and sometimes edged with gold, or silver, or Bone, that is, Pillow lace. For the ruffs, one cannot but wonder at the skill of the starcher who, even with the aid of a wire frame, could stiffen so large a surface of such delicate materials so as to make them retain the required shape even for a few hours of a damp English day. But it is on this account that we have now to depend almost entirely on the pictorial art for our information about them. Starch

Illustration VIII.

Venetian Rose Point.

and constant wear have been too much for the fine "lawne cut-work," and lace-trimmed ruffs have, with scarcely any exception, long since perished with their wearers.

It is at this point that the large collection of pattern books which have been preserved to us from the sixteenth and seventeenth centuries are of great interest. They became possible after the art of printing became popular, and they range in point of date from the *Livre nouveau*, published in Cologne in 1527, to the *Méthode pour faire une infinité de desseins par le Rev. Père Sebastien Truchet*, published in Paris in 1722.

A list of these books, preserved in various European libraries, is to be found in the Appendix to Mrs. Palliser's *History of Lace*. A few original copies are in the National Art Library, South Kensington, and a considerable number of such as were of Venetian origin have been recently reproduced in modern facsimile editions by that energetic publisher, Signor Oncagnia, of Venice. These can be seen and studied in the library of the British Museum, so that this interesting subject is now brought within easy reach of the English student.

The earliest of these books refer to embroidery in gold and silver and silks, as well as in thread. In 1548, one published in Venice by Mathio Pagan, *Il specchio di pensieri delle belle e virtudiose donne* ("the mirror of the thoughts of beautiful and virtuous ladies"), gives patterns of "punti tagliati," "punti gropposi e punti in Stuora"—Cut-work, Knotted-work, and Embroidered netting. Ten years later, in 1558, the same author brought out *La gloria et l'honore di punti tagliati e punti in aere* ("the glory and the honour of Cut-work and Open-work"). And this allusion to "punto in Aria" is very interesting as fixing the date of the introduction of so important an innovation in lace-making.

The early style of these patterns is narrow and wiry, corresponding closely to the edgings of the frills shown in contemporary pictures; but soon the designs become richer and wider, and being worked in finer thread than that formerly used for the old linen lace-work, and combined with bands of Reticella, produce a very handsome as well as light and open effect.

In James the First's reign some concession was made to comfort, and the same fluted and starched ruff was allowed to fall towards the shoulders instead of standing out round the head; then suddenly the full frill gave way to the "Col rabattu," the large falling collar with the lace border of Charles the First's time so familiar to us in Vandyke's portraits of that monarch.

But to return to "Punto in Aria" and its developments. The various Laces which owe their invention to this origin are known to us as Point lace. The great distinction between them and the Lace we have hitherto considered is that Point lace is worked with button-hole stitch alone (in Italian, "Punto a festone"). In the preceding Laces, as shown in Illustration I., Fig. 5, sewing over, rope stitch, and the in-and-out stitch called "Punto di Genoa" are also used, but in the later Point lace these are discarded and the Lace is made entirely with button-hole stitch, close or open. All the varied effects we so much admire are produced by this alone.

Lace so worked had its origin and chief centre in Venice, and it is to be remarked that like our own English manufactures, it was brought to perfection not by any State encouragement such as government schools or protective duties, but rather in spite of sumptuary laws, and by the enterprise and artistic instincts of private citizens. It culminated in the splendid Lace known in French and English by many names, but called in Italian collectively "Punto tagliato a foliami," or simply "Punto di Venezia."

This Lace had an astonishing success in Italy and also in Spain and France. In the latter country especially enormous quantities of it were lavished on the dress both of men and women. Owing, as it is said, to the long curls of the young King Louis the Fourteenth, falling collars had gone out of fashion, ponderous wigs were worn by the courtiers in imitation of the King's natural locks, and, to suit the new style of coiffure, cambric neckties with falling ends of the richest Venetian Point lace were adopted. And not only so was this Lace used, but the gentlemen's sleeve cuffs, the ends of their waist scarves, the canons or frills half a yard in width which finished the short breeches of the day, the rosettes of their shoes, and even the tops of their high leather boots, were most inappropriately decorated in the same manner.

The ladies wore the beautiful "Punto di Venezia" on their caps, their sleeves, and their aprons, besides using it, as we see in contemporary pictures, to trim their dinner table-covers and pillow-cases, and even as coverlets for their beds, where, it must be remembered, they used to hold receptions of their friends, male and female. For church purposes it was

Illustration IX.

Flat Venetian Point.

also largely used. There is a superb altar frontal at the South Kensington Museum made entirely of Venetian Point, and in a case close by it a cardinal's alb of pleated linen, trimmed with a flounce half a yard in width of the finest "Punto tagliato a foliami," or Rose Point.

In England we have the evidence of the actual Lace worn by Charles the Second himself—and it is still preserved on his funeral effigy in Westminster Abbey—to prove to us that the finest Venetian Point was also in fashion here. The Lace is very beautiful, now mouldering away into dust and ashes together with a truly strange collection, mementoes of bygone rank and splendour.

Venetian Point is variously called Raised Venetian Point or Gros Point de Venise, also Rose Point, Carnival Lace, Cardinal's, and sometimes even Pope's Point, Point Plat de Venise, Point d'Espagne or Guipure, and all these names have been used somewhat indiscriminately. For the two last, Guipure denotes Lace made with braid, or tape, or gimp, and is not in any way applicable to fine Needle-point. Point d'Espagne is clearly a misnomer for work which, though it may have been occasionally produced in Spain under Italian influence, was certainly of Venetian origin. On this more will be said under the head of Spanish Lace. For the rest, as it is certain that different stages of development and decline can be observed in the history of Venetian Lace, and having explained that the names usually employed are not always clearly separable, it has been thought best here to make use only of such names as will serve to mark the distinction between three separate stages in point of date and style of the Lace known as a whole as "Punto tagliato a foliami" or Venetian Point.

Illustration X.

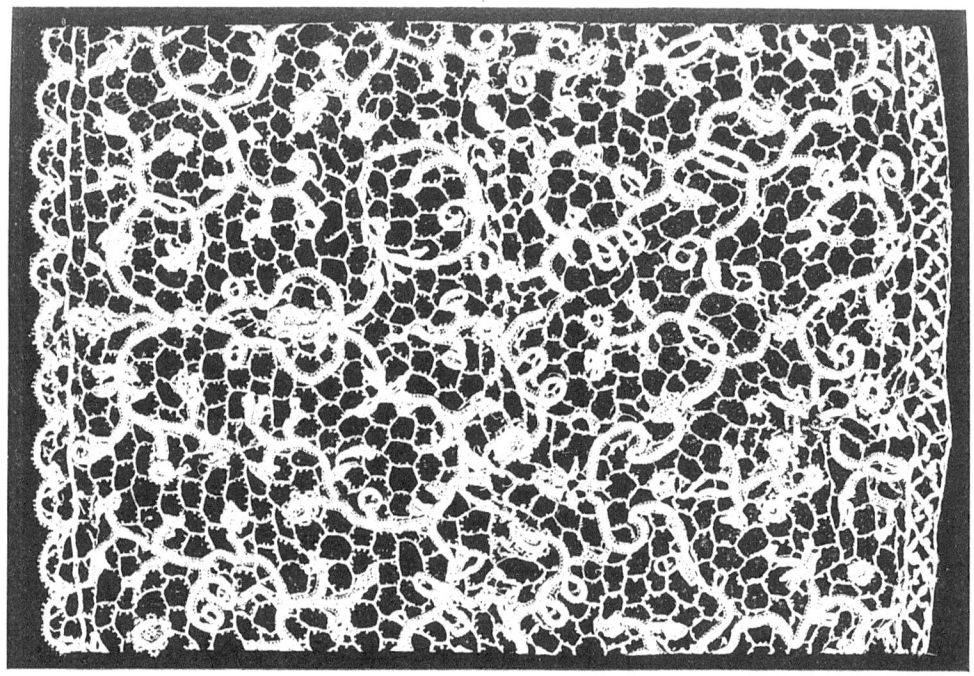

Venetian Point (Coraline), or Punto di Venezia.

We would class them thus:—

1. Venetian Raised Point (*Fr.* Gros Point de Venise), under which head we include the variety called Rose Point.

2. Venetian Flat Point (*Fr.* Point Plat de Venise), with its later variety which, from its appearance, we would call Coraline Point.

3. Grounded Venetian Point (*Fr.* Point de Venise à réseau), and in this class we include "Punto di Burano," so called from the island, near Venice, where it was made; the last and final stage of the Art at the close of the eighteenth century.

Raised Point, or Gros Point De Venise

The principal distinctions of Raised Venetian Point are: First, the boldness and continuity of the designs, which sometimes extend throughout a whole piece of Lace; Secondly, the "cordonnet," which is very prominent. It is thickened in parts by the addition of sheaves of thread closely overcast with button-hole stitches, and often edged with rows of "picots." The Lace is held together by "brides," but only so far as is necessary for strength, the "bride"-work forming no essential part of the general design. The splendid specimen reproduced in Illustration VII. is in the South Kensington Museum, and forms part of the unrivalled collection of Lace bequeathed to the nation by the late Mrs. Bolckow. Such Lace has been fitly called the crowning triumph of the work of the needle. The freedom and beauty of the design are as remarkable as the exquisite delicacy and variety of the details and the perfect skill of their execution. An Italian poet is said to have described such work as "scolpito in relievo" (sculptured in relief). The words remind one that Venetian Lace in its prime was produced when manual skill had reached its highest point and went hand in hand with the heaven-born instinct of beauty; when, in fact, the spirit of the Renaissance had infused life and vigour into every form of Art throughout Italy, and when the workers in gold and enamel, in wood and iron, and even in silk and linen thread, were artists as well as the sculptor and the painter. Such periods are short-lived.

Rose Point

The distinctions to be drawn between this and the preceding Lace are not very marked; the style is modified, not changed. The designs are composed on a smaller scale, enriching ornament is more abundant, and the groundwork of "brides" becomes a more important element in the whole effect. These are now further decorated not only with "picots" but also with numerous little whirls and rosettes, and hence perhaps the name of Rose Point. The specimen shown in Illustration VIII. is also, like the preceding, taken from the Bolckow bequest in the South Kensington Museum, and is a singularly rich example. Here the raised "cordonnet" is edged not only with one but with two and three rows of loops and "picots," till the effect produced is almost that of snowflakes, on which account such Lace is sometimes called "Point de neige." Rose Point is later in style than the "Gros Point de Venise."

Flat Venetian Point

The name of this Lace denotes the difference of its character. The raised work is here altogether absent, the designs, though often very graceful and well composed, as is the case with the specimen shown in Illustration IX., are more attenuated than in Raised Point, while the "brides," as in Rose Point, are an important feature in the general effect.

The manner in which the work was executed was the same in all three. The piece of parchment on which the pattern was drawn out was tacked upon some thick, soft cloth, then a coarse thread or cord was sewn down along the outline through both the parchment and the cloth together. The scroll-work or flowers of the pattern were then filled in with button-hole stitches, as shown in Fig. i, Illustration I., either close or open, and finally the "brides" were added to hold the parts of the pattern together, and when the work was completed a sharp knife was passed between the parchment and cloth to cut the stitches which held down the outline cord and so to free the finished Lace without any risk of injuring it. A later style of Flat Venetian Point is one that we venture to name on account of its strong resemblance to the delicate fretwork of fine coral growths, and also because of the story that is told of its origin,

Coraline Point

It is said that a young girl, a lace-worker in Venice, received as a parting gift from her sailor lover when he left her to wait for his return, a branch of coraline, and she, looking

Illustration XI.

Grounded Venetian Point.

at it and thinking of him while at her work, considered how she could imitate it with her needle. She tried, and the result was so charming that she speedily found imitators, and the Lace became one of the most favourite in use. This Lace is often specially called "Venetian Point," and rightly so, for whereas the "Point Plat" and the "Gros Point" have been copied both in Spain and France, this Lace, whose origin is a gift from the sea, has never been produced elsewhere than on the shores of the Adriatic. But beautiful and wonderful as it is, it must he considered as a decline from the earlier styles. Very little connected pattern is to be traced in it at all, and what there is is often shapeless and angular. There is little or no raised work; the ground of "brides picotées," though well distributed, is without method in its arrangement and the shape of the meshes. It has, in fact, the effect of a tangle—a work of nature rather than of Art, charming for its delicate workmanship, and for the very reason of its confusion. But the finest Art has never been considered to be the mere imitation of the free growth of natural plants or animals, its object is rather to generalise and idealise nature, and to express and suggest, through the representation of things familiar to us, the higher spirit of symmetry and harmony, and that sense of ideal beauty which is the peculiar gift of artistic genius.

The third and last stage of Venetian Lace is the

Grounded Point
(*Fr.* Point de Venise à réseau.)

Till about the middle of the seventeenth century there was an almost insatiable demand for Venetian Lace at the French Court, and the supply seems to have been abundant; but when the manufactures of Alençon and the neighbourhood were started, encouraged by the King, and protected by prohibitive duties against the importation of Italian Lace, the profits of the Venetian lace-makers fell off considerably. It was then that, in the hope of retaining their foreign customers, they learnt a lesson from their supplanters, and in imitation of the manufactures of Alençon they adopted the "réseau" ground. The style of the "réseau" is much the same as the French, though the mesh is rounder and does not fall into lines across the Lace as with Alençon and Burano. It is composed, however, of double twisted threads throughout, as Fig. 3, Illustration I. This Lace differs further from Alençon in that the pattern is not outlined with any "cordonnet." Venetian Grounded Point is a very beautiful piece of work, exquisitely fine, delicate and graceful (see Illustration XI.), yet in point of style it falls under the strictures passed on the Rococo period, inasmuch as it often suffers from a redundancy of ill-arranged decoration.

The variety and abundance of the ornamental "à jours" are especially to be noticed. These are far too numerous to be described, but a zigzag ornament may be specified as very characteristic. The pattern usually includes the representation of lilies and other natural flowers, and the edge of the Lace is generally in the form of a shallow scollop, arranged so as to form part of the design.

This Lace was produced during the latter half of the eighteenth century; then came the end, when the storm of the French Revolution burst upon Europe and overwhelmed the Venetian Republic in its course. Rich patrons had then to think of saving their lives and what they could of their property, and no longer bought Lace, and the poorer classes learnt by experience that to kill the goose who lays the golden eggs is not the way to prosperity.

Yet the manufacture survived for a little while longer in the island of Burano, near Venice, and as late as the beginning of the nineteenth century a needle-made Lace, insignificant in pattern and coarse in execution, was still made there by native workers. Mrs. Palliser, in her *History of Lace*, published in 1864, gives an illustration of a specimen of Burano Lace which she says had been bought of an old woman, the maker, one Ceccia la Scarpariola, the last survivor of the lace-making industry, and she adds, "Venice Point is now no more."

Illustration XII.

Old Burano Point.

This same Ceccia or Cencia was still older when in 1872 an unusually severe winter reduced the inhabitants of Burano to great straits of poverty. The population was at the time entirely dependent on fishery for the means of existence, and when the canals and lagoons were for weeks covered with ice, wholesale starvation seemed imminent. Their distress came to the knowledge of a M. Paulo Fambri, who made an appeal to the charitable throughout Italy for help. The King and Queen and the Pope gave the example, and a considerable sum was raised, part of which was immediately spent in alleviating the distress, and with what remained, as a more permanent source of help and comfort to these poor people, a school was started in which it was hoped that the lost Art of lace-making, so profitable in the past, might be revived for their benefit. Cencia Scarpariola was then seventy years of age, and was the only living person who remembered or could show how the work was done, and she, from old age and infirmity, was incapable of teaching. However, nothing daunted, some Venetian ladies, headed by the Countess Adriana Marcello, who eventually assumed the whole management of the affair, succeeded in finding an intelligent worker who could learn only by seeing the old woman at her needle, and she in turn taught others. Keeping at first to the old Burano style, and afterwards copying

Point and Pillow Lace

from patterns and designs which were most kindly lent by Her Majesty the Queen of Italy and others, the school has at length been able to produce Lace of various kinds, but little inferior to the best of the Venetian triumphs of former days.

In Needle-point lace the Burano girls now reproduce Raised Venetian Point, Point d'Argentan, and d'Alençon, and old Brussels, as well as the peculiar Burano Lace of their native island. Thus a beautiful Art has been successfully saved from oblivion, and as the lace-makers are able to earn what to those simple folk is very good wages, the means of subsistence of the population is very considerably increased, and comfort and good morals are the satisfactory results.

In an account of Venetian lace-making, written by Urbani Gheltof, published in Venice, and translated into English by Lady Layard, a very detailed description, accompanied by diagrams, is given of the mode of execution of Burano Point.

From this it appears that it is usually worked on a pillow, not however, of course, with bobbins as for pillow-lace. The object of the pillow or bolster is merely to raise the work to a suitable height on the lap of the lace-maker and to diminish the necessity of much handling. On the middle of the upper side of the pillow there rests a small wooden cylinder across which the parchment pattern is stretched, leaving an open space under it for the convenience of the worker; thus the strip of Lace is kept smooth and flat. In working the "réseau" ground a thread is fixed straight across the whole width of the Lace as a foundation for each row of meshes, being passed through and fastened to any sprig or part of the pattern which may intervene, and on this thread the looped meshes are worked. The result is the formation of a remarkably square-shaped mesh, and by this, and also by the streaky and cloudy appearance of the "réseau," Burano Point may be recognised; the latter effect is owing to unevenness in the quality of the thread. Burano also differs from Alençon in that its "cordonnet" is not overcast or covered with button-hole stitch, but is only stitched down round the outline. In the matter of design the patterns are generally, as in the illustration, small and floral, the "réseau" ground being sprinkled with leaflets or blossoms; but Alençon patterns of a late period were also often copied, so that the quality of the "réseau," and especially the heavy thread "cordonnet," should be chiefly relied upon rather than the pattern as marking the difference between the two kinds of Lace.

For the benefit of visitors to Venice it may be added that the Burano Lace schools, under the patronage of the Queen of Italy, are in the Palazzo Municipale, opposite the church in the principal Piazza, in the island, and that they will well repay a visit. Lace-making can be better understood by being seen than by even the most careful of descriptions.

Of Spanish Laces

These are included in the present chapter on account of the frequent misuse of the terms "Spanish Point" and "Point d'Espagne" applied to Italian Laces. As in the case of the Brussels Lace known as "Point d'Angleterre," names may be in common use and yet not always safe guides. With regard to Spanish Lace it seems difficult to be sure of the facts of the case.

It is certain that great quantities of Lace that we should describe as Raised Venetian Point were used in Spain both for the dress of the Court and also especially for the adornment of the church vestments, altars, and images of saints. During the French invasion, when churches and monasteries were freely pillaged, these treasures were scattered over the world, and on this account, if for no other reason, were sold in the market as "Spanish Lace." But it is also probably true that Lace of the kind was made in the convents of Spain, where nuns from Italy would naturally teach and introduce an Art so much in request. To judge, however, by style where the actual nationality of the work seems doubtful, it is clear that there is no sufficient difference to mark "Point d'Espagne" as a really distinct Lace from Venetian Point.

The Lace known for certain to be of Spanish production is a coarse pillow Guipure both of white thread and also of gold and silver. This is a loose fabric made of three "cordonnets," the centre one being the coarsest, held together with finer threads running in and out across them, and with "brides" to connect and keep the pattern in shape.

Black and white Blonde has during this century been also much made in Catalonia for that graceful national head-dress, the mantilla, but it is not at all equal in quality to similar Lace made in the north of France, of which more will be said further on. In fact Spaniards, though they have always been very good customers for the Lace of other countries, do not appear at any time to have been great Lace producers.

Of Italian Pillow Lace

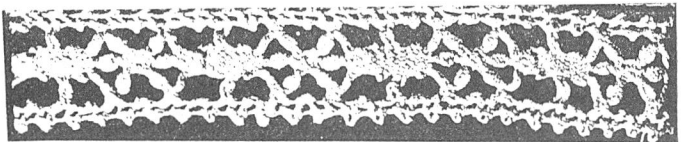

Genoese Plaited Lace.

Before entering into details concerning Lace that will fall under the above description, some mention must be made of a decorative work of very ancient origin, namely:

Punto à Groppo, or Knotted Lace
(Now known as Macramé.)

This must be considered as a very early form of Pillow lace, being made with interlaced threads on a pillow, though by knotting and not by plaiting as in the modern Pillow lace. It no doubt grew out of the knotted fringes that we see represented in Byzantine mosaics, or it may claim a still earlier origin in the same fringes as represented in ancient Assyrian sculpture. During the sixteenth century much of this work was produced in Genoa, but the effect was necessarily stiff and heavy and was not found suitable for other than church and household purposes.

The specimen shown in Illustration XIII. was bought in Italy some fifty years ago, but the work since then has been introduced into this country, and so many books of patterns and directions have been published that any detailed description of it seems unnecessary here. The name "Macramé" by which it has been known to us, is as modern as its revival; it comes from an Arabic word signifying an ornamental trimming.

It is interesting to notice that as we have seen that the looped stitch of netting was the first starting-point of the needlework button-hole stitch, with which all Point laces are made, so we may consider these knotted fringes as the beginning from which all the future Pillow lace work was developed.

Great rivalry exists between Italy and Belgium as to which of the two may claim the merit of the invention of Pillow lace. While Belgium, as we have seen, can refer to the picture by Quintin Matsys of the girl with the Lace pillow as a proof that the Art existed in the north as early as the end of the fifteenth century, Italy can show on her part the

Illustration XIII.

Macramé, or Punto a Groppo.

pattern-book for Pillow lace-making preserved in the Museum of the Arsenal at Venice, entitled, *Le Pompe*, and dated 1557, and if this later date should be quoted as antagonistic to her contention, it may be fairly allowed that an Art must have been already some time in existence before it could have created a literature.

M. Seguin, favouring the Italian view, is of opinion that the Art spread from Italy through France to Belgium by means of travelling pedlars who, journeying slowly across Europe and stopping everywhere on their road to sell their wares, carried the knowledge of Lace-making into the Flemish provinces, where the population was already familiar with, and skilful in, the manufacture of linen. However that may be, it is certain that Pillow laces of the Italian sort, known to us as

Illustration XIV.

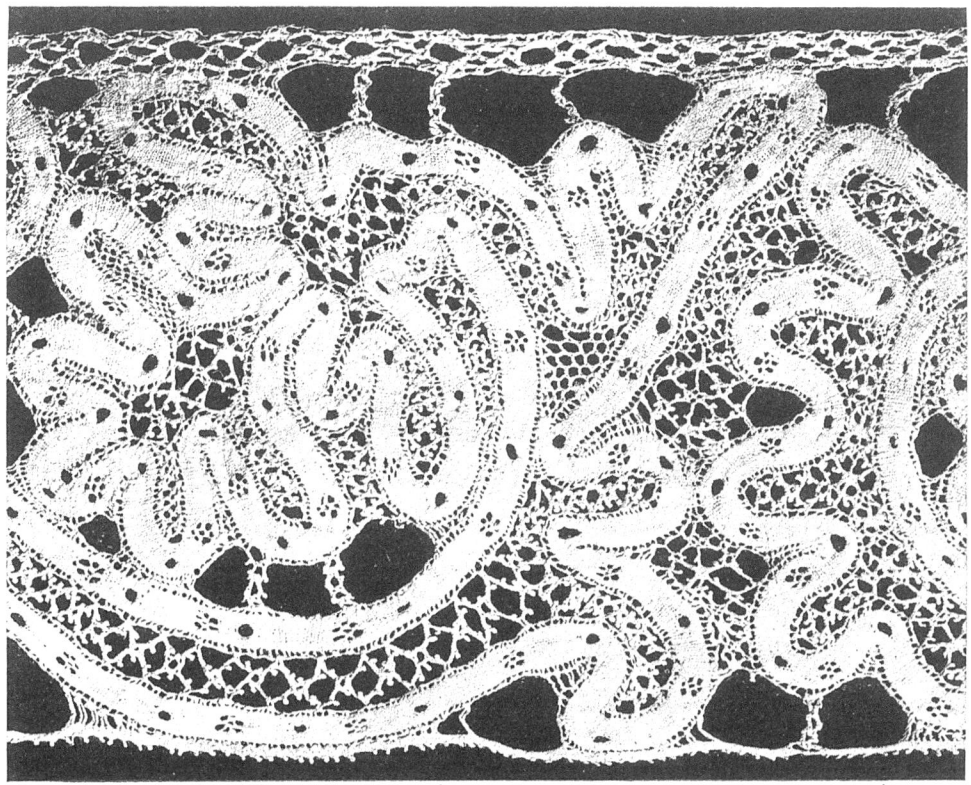

Pillow Guipure.

Pillow Guipure,

seem to have been among the earliest made both in Flanders and in Italy, and that in style of design they have a distinctly Italian character. It is this Lace about which the authorities at South Kensington decide to be doubtful. One must conclude that they have good authority for believing that what would certainly from its appearance pass for Italian Lace has actually often been made in Flanders. They have therefore labelled the cases containing it as "Flemish or Italian." If a distinctive difference may be suggested between Lace of the same style of pattern made in the two countries, it would appear perhaps to be in the quality of the thread. As has been said, the inhabitants of the Flemish provinces have always been noted for their superior skill in spinning and weaving linen, and whether from lack of such skill or from a difference in national taste, there is no doubt that Italian Lace generally of all kinds is heavier and stouter in character than that produced in the north of Europe. Illustrations XIV. and XXIX. should be compared.

Pillow Guipure may be described as composed of a tape, made on the pillow so as to follow the curves of the pattern and connected by "brides" also made on the pillow, that is, made of twisted or plaited threads, not as in Needle lace covered with buttonhole

Illustration XV.

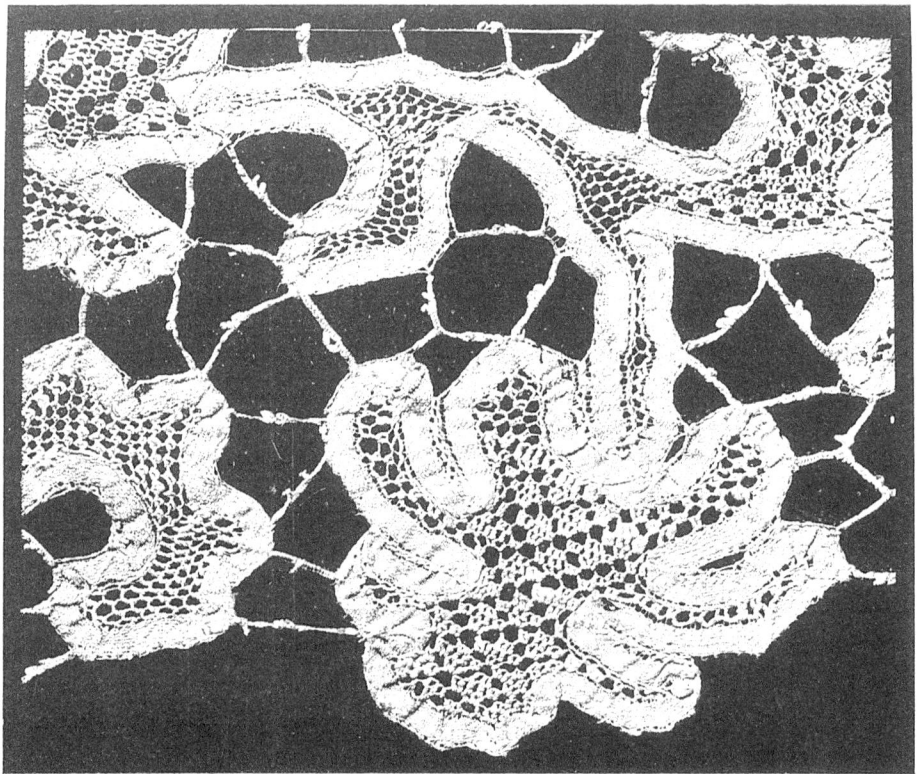

Mixed Guipure made with a Woven Tape.

stitches. The "brides" are sometimes ornamented with "picots," and the open spaces are filled in with "à jours," also pillow-worked.

This Lace, though flat, is, from its excellent designs of a bold Renaissance character and its good workmanship, often very handsome in appearance.

A variety on this is the mixed Needle and Pillow lace, called

Mezzo Punto
(*Fr.* Point de Canaille.)

In this the "à jours" and "brides picotées" are worked in needle stitches and complete in Point the pattern traced out with Pillow-made tape. Sometimes this mixed Guipure is grounded with a coarse needle-made "réseau" instead of "brides," but whether so or with "brides," it is too often made not with tape worked to the pattern on the pillow, as is the wholly Pillow Guipure, but with a woven tape made first separately and then tacked on to the pattern as outlined on parchment; the result is that clumsy puckers and folds spoil the turns and curves of the design, a defect, as we all know, which has been faithfully copied in the modern revival of the Lace. Whether owing to this or to the mixture of methods, or

Illustration XVI.

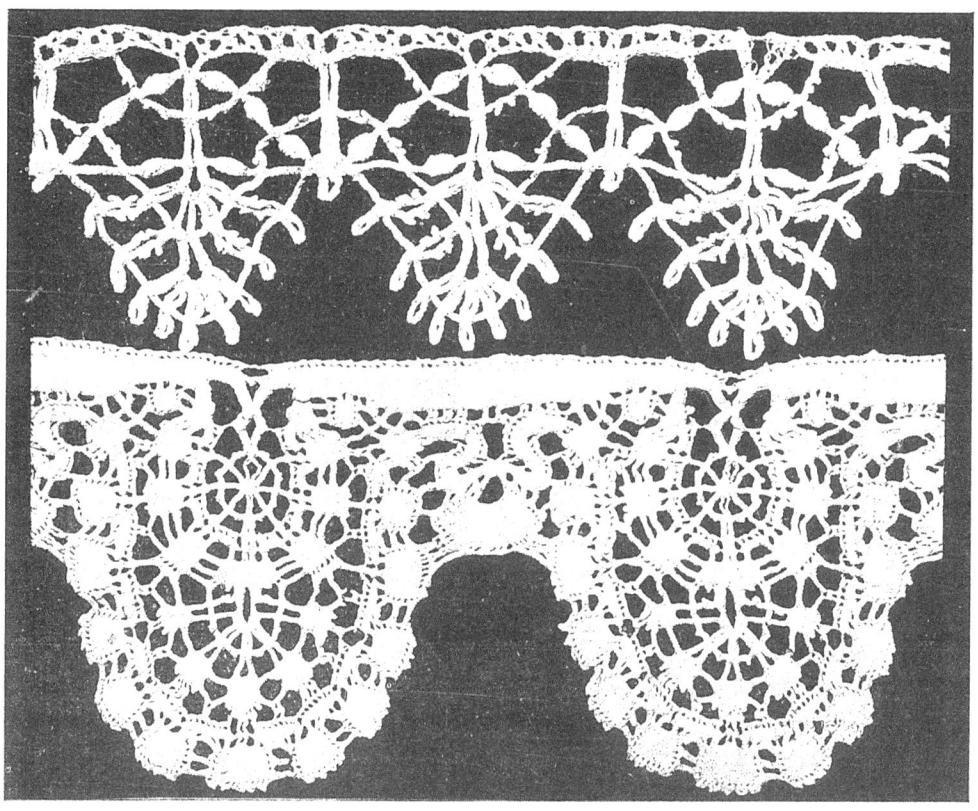

1. Genoese Plaited Lace.   2. Genoese Collar Lace

to faults of design, the Mezzo Punto never has the simple, free effect of the Pillow Guipure, and is very far from attaining to the richness of Needle Point.

It has been said, though with what amount of truth we do not know, that this Lace originated in Naples, and was meant to supply the poorer folk with a cheap imitation of the rich Point laces worn by the Court. There seems no doubt that both mixed Lace and Pillow Guipure were intended to copy the Venetian Points, and from being easier to work, and less costly to purchase, they gained favour very rapidly.

Genoese Lace
(*It*. Punto di Genoa.)

As Venice was the great centre for Needle-point, so was Genoa for Pillow lace-making in Italy, and during the greater part of the seventeenth century a constant supply was produced in that town and its neighbourhood of the handsome vandyked and scolloped border Lace, called from the use to which it was put, Collar lace. In the pictures of Rubens and Vandyke we see it frequently represented as trimming the broad falling linen collars both of men and of elderly ladies.

Illustration XVII.

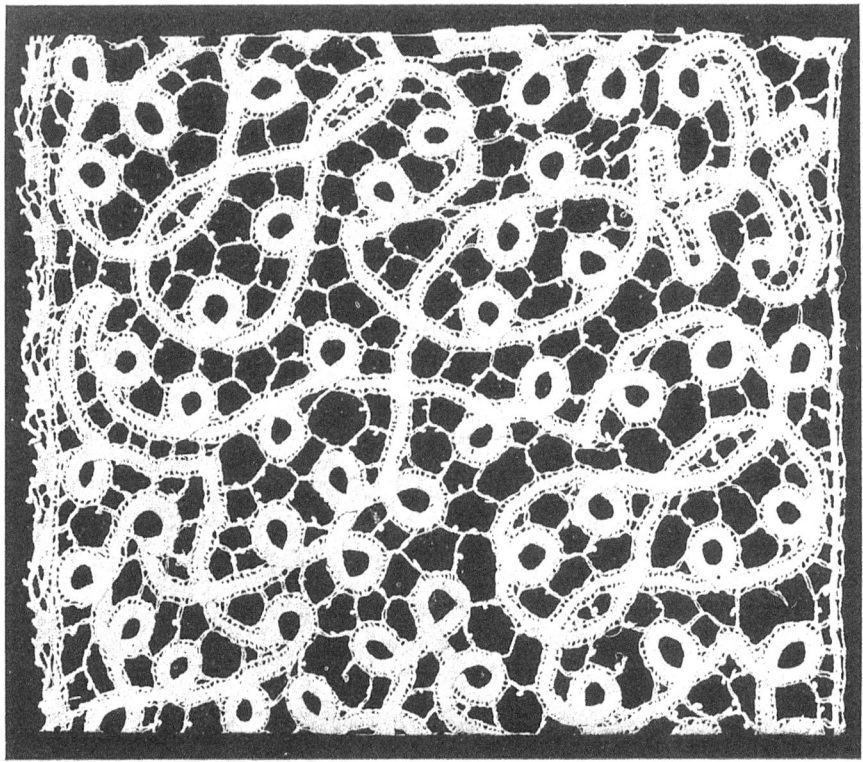

Genoese Tape Guipure.

The younger ladies also made great use of it as trimming for the shoulders of their *décolleté* dresses, and also for sleeves, aprons, etc. It can be distinguished from Flemish Lace, also employed in the same way, by its greater boldness of design.

Collar Lace

Collar Lace is of two kinds, both of which are represented in Illustration XVI. That of which No. 2 is a specimen resembles in principle the Pillow Guipure already described. A scroll-like pattern, as of tape, is turned and twisted into forms of considerable elegance which at the same time compose the deep scollop of the required shape. This Lace is round and not pointed in its outline. The whole is strengthened and connected by short "brides."

Plaited Lace
(*Fr*. Point de Gènes frisé. *It*. Merletto a piombini.)

No. 1 is generally pointed or vandyked in shape, and is worked in a somewhat unusual manner; the Lace is made entirely with plaits of four threads each, following the design,

Illustration XVIII.

Milanese Pillow Lace.

and with little oval enlargements resembling ears of wheat, which are sometimes arranged as beads on a thread and sometimes composed into trefoils or quatrefoils, or spokes radiating from a common centre.

Genoese Tape Guipure

Besides the border Lace chiefly used for trimming collars which has been already described, a Lace sometimes known as Tape Guipure is also attributed to Genoa. A specimen is shown in Illustration XVII. which will sufficiently explain the name. A convoluted tape, but made to its shape on the pillow with no unseemly puckers or folds, seems to wind for ever through the design. Great ingenuity is shown in the even and well-balanced distribution of the pattern, if pattern it can be called, where so little order or intention can be traced. With the enrichment of numerous "picots," and also sometimes of ornamental "à jours" filling in the looped spaces, this Lace has often a very good though

Illustration XIX.

Italian Peasant Lace (three specimens).

perhaps monotonous effect. It has been much used for church vestments, and was frequently of considerable width.

Punto Di Milano
(*Eng.* Milanese Pillow lace.)

It is needless to say that neither this Lace nor "Punto di Genoa" are rightly called "Punti" or Needle-point lace; they are both made on the pillow. The name "Punto di Milano" is, however, so commonly known in connection with it, that it would be pedantic not to recognise it, though with a protest. It was like the preceding Laces, of Genoese origin, but has survived till recent times in Cantu, near Milan. It is by far the most beautiful, as well as the best known of Italian Pillow laces. It much resembles the Genoese

Tape Guipure, but with far less of monotony, and much more of graceful design in the style of its patterns. In some fine specimens, such as that represented in Illustration XVIII., coats of arms are often introduced, probably when the piece of Lace was made by order of some prelate or personage of noble family; but as a rule easy-flowing scroll-work fills up the composition. This is the only Italian Pillow lace which is grounded with "réseau," a fact that marks it as relatively late in point of date.

It is somewhat singular that this "réseau" should very much resemble that of Valenciennes, having a diamond-shaped mesh formed with a plait of four threads (See Fig. 7, Illustration II.), though the two kinds of Lace are in other respects of totally different construction. In "Punto di Milano," as will be easily seen by referring to the illustration, the pattern is made first on the pillow by itself, and the "réseau" ground is worked in round it afterwards, sloping in all directions so as to fit into the spaces; while Valenciennes is worked all in one piece on the pillow, pattern and "réseau" together.

The difference here noticed forms a very marked distinction between two kinds of Pillow lace, one of which seems to have originated in the Pillow Guipures that we have been considering, which in the case of "Punto di Milano" were afterwards, so to speak, fitted with a "réseau" ground; the other kind is represented in Italy by the various peasant Laces, of which three specimens are given in Illustration XIX. These are worked all in one piece, with one set of threads, forming as it were the woof and warp of the material. This can be almost verified by a close examination of the facsimile print (notice No. 2), though of course more certainly with the actual Lace. No. 1 is worked in the same manner as the plaited Genoese Collar lace, that is, with plaited threads in sets of four. The designs of these peasant Laces are often very good, though the thread with which they are made is coarse, and their general effect thick. They were chiefly used for household purposes.

Some thirty or forty years ago, before the time when railroads had become universal in Italy, and when the traveller was fain to rumble along during a three or four days' journey in *vetturino* between Rome and Florence or Naples, the rough country inns at which he stopped for the night no doubt left much to be desired in the way of good food, cleanliness, and comfort; but if he could take it as a consolation, the silk hangings of his bed, his sheets and pillow-case, his towels and tablecloth, were nearly sure to be adorned with this strong and probably home-made country Lace. He soon found, moreover, that after the indispensable bargaining enjoyed by both parties alike, he could, for a very reasonable consideration, make the Lace his own. So the dirt and discomfort are forgotten, and the recollection of the amusing incident, together with the Lace, remains. It is now no longer made, nor is any more of it to be bought.

Maltese Lace

A notice of this Lace is added to this chapter because of its very strong resemblance to, and probable development from, the Genoese manufacture. Mrs. Bury Palliser, in her *History of Lace*, gives a sketch of a representation of Lace copied from a Cardinal's monument in the church of St. John in Valetta, from which it would seem that the wavy character of the designs of recent Maltese Lace may possibly be of ancient origin. But there

Illustration XX.

Maltese Lace (Black and White Silk).

seems no doubt that a great improvement took place both in its designs and execution in consequence of the efforts of Lady Hamilton Chichester, who, in 1833, brought lace-workers over from Genoa to teach their craft in the island. The Lace is made in white thread and in black and white silk; in the white silk specimen shown in Illustration XX. the little wheat-ear ornament so characteristic of Genoa is clearly seen.

Of French Laces

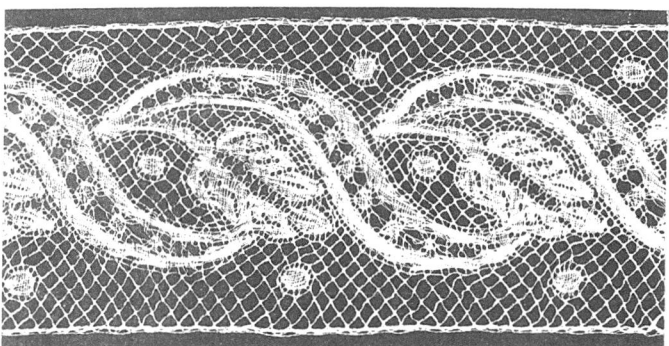

Modern Valenciennes.

Point d'Alençon

It is said that Needle-point lace was made at Alençon as early as 1650 or thereabouts, but though mention has been found of it by name at that time, it did not attain to any great perfection or celebrity till the manufacture was taken up and encouraged by Colbert, the well-known minister under Louis the Fourteenth. True to the principles that have governed French policy in commercial matters to this day, great jealousy and annoyance had long been felt by the various ministers of the crown at the large sums of money yearly spent upon the importation of Venetian and other Italian Laces, then thought an indispensable part of the dress of the Court. Repeated sumptuary laws were passed to check the trade, but fashion is stronger than laws, and as, judging by their portraits, the royal family themselves were among the chief culprits, these naturally had but little effect. To one issued in 1660 we owe an amusing satire called "La Révolte des Passemens," passement (Gimp or Guipure) being the old French word including Lace and embroideries. The various Laces enumerated, "Poincts de Gènes, de Raguse, de Venise, d'Angleterre et de Flandres," down to the humble "Gueuse," the equivalent of the modern Torchon, are supposed to assemble and to make indignant lamentation over their exclusion from Court. The poem is dedicated to Mademoiselle de la Trousse, and it is supposed to have been written by someone belonging to the circle of Madame de Sevigné. The wit is perhaps a little laboured. The gist of it is as follows:—

One of the Laces addressing the rest with some warmth, says:—

Illustration XXI.

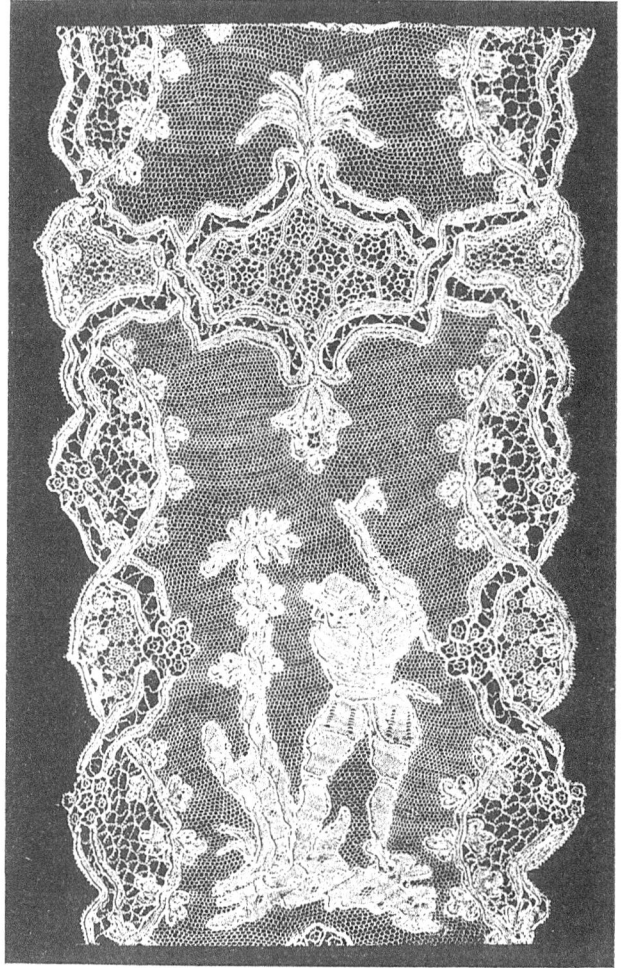

A Lappet, Point d'Alençon.

"Dites moi je vous en prie
Poincts, dentelles ou broderies
Qu'aurons nous donc fait à la court
Pour qu'on nous chasse haut et court," etc.

To which "une Grande Dentelle d'Angleterre" replies:—

"Cet infortune sans seconde
Me fait bien renoncer au monde.
   * * * *
Pour ne plus tourner à tout vent
Comme d'entrer dans un Couvent."

Illustration XXII.

1. Early Point d'Alençon. 2. Later Point d'Alençon.

But the Laces of Flanders will not patiently submit to be so extinguished, and many angry verses ensue. At last a "Dentelle noire" in despair hires itself out to a game merchant for nets to catch snipe and the rest:—

"Chacun dissimulant sa rage
Doucement pliait son bagage."
    * * * *

when "une pauvre malheureuse la Gueuse" (it was the Lace of the common people) declares that she at least will not give in, and that if they will follow her lead she will certainly replace them in their former position.

Illustration XXIII.

Point d'Argentan.

"La dessus le Poinct d'Alençon
Ayant bien appris la leçon
Fit une fort belle harangue,"

and the result was that they all repaired to the Fair of St. Germains prepared to do battle for their rights. However, the King brought down his big guns and the brave Laces forthwith took to their heels. They were condemned at a court-martial, some to be made into tinder for the sole use of the King's mousquetaires, and others to be sent to the galleys or burned alive; but Cupid, "le petit dieu plein de finesse," makes intercession and they are forgiven and received again into royal favour.

The poem is also interesting as giving us the names of the Laces most in repute at the time. "Point de Raguse" is not easy to identify. Ragusa is a town on the Dalmatian coast, and being near to the Venetian dominions, though not at the time included in them, the Lace was probably of much the same kind as that produced in Venice itself; if so, its fame is at present extinguished by that of its more powerful neighbour.

The edict against Lace must have made a great impression on society, for Abraham Bosse, whose contemporary engravings are a mine of information concerning the dress and manners of the day, gives us an amusing record of the crisis. He depicts the despair of the lady of fashion now attired Puritan-wise in plain hemmed linen cuffs, collar and cap, as she mournfully packs away all her rich lace-rimmed costumes, and bewails her sad fate in heartbroken verses.

The failure of past edicts was, however, the immediate cause of a great success. In order to exclude foreign manufactures Colbert hit upon the better plan of encouraging

Illustration XXIV.

1. Early Valenciennes.   2. Later Valenciennes.

those of his own country. He induced Venetian lace-workers to settle near his daughter-in-law's castle of Lonray at Alençon, and selected a competent directrice in one Catherine de Marcq, and finally in 1665 a flourishing Lace factory was established, and Lace was produced in exact imitation of Venetian Point, which rivalled if it did not surpass the Italian original.

It was called by Royal Decree "Point de France." The name lasted in connection with Alençon Lace till about 1790. It is impossible now to distinguish the earliest Lace so called and produced in Alençon from the finest Venetian Point. The designs are in the same style, and the workmanship is extremely beautiful; but by degrees, as greater freedom was very wisely allowed to the workers, a new and separate style developed itself. The patterns became smaller and more delicate, finer thread was employed than that made use of in Italy, "brides" became closer and more regular in arrangement, and finally the needlework "réseau" ground was invented in imitation of the Pillow laces of the neighbouring Flemish Provinces, and we see attained in perfection the style of Lace now known as Point d'Alençon.

The Needle-point "réseau" was worked at Alençon about the year 1717, but combined with it the patterns still retained a strong Renaissance character. Running scroll-like bands

Illustration XXV.

A Lappet, Early Valenciennes.

filled in with fanciful "à jours" are a special characteristic of this period; they wave from side to side of the piece of Lace, form part of the edge and enclose spaces which are decorated with flower forms conventionally treated. (See Fig. 2, Illustration XXII.)

A variety of this style is to be met with which has sometimes been distinguished as a separate Lace under the name of "Argentella." Its peculiarity is a large and very ornamental honeycomb filling, made use of alternately with the ordinary "réseau" as a groundwork for the design, with a very beautiful effect. Mrs. Bury Palliser mentions that some of it was sent to her from Genoa, but most authorities seem agreed that it is undoubtedly Point d'Alençon.

Towards the beginning of Louis the Sixteenth's reign Alençon patterns were much modified, the flower representations became more and more naturalistic (see the beautiful representation of roses in Fig. 1 of the illustration), and the groundwork was sprinkled

Illustration XXVI.

1. Point de Paris.   2. Lille

with spots or leaves. Finally under the Empire the last stage was reached, the pattern dwindled and became little more than an outline of "cordonnet," and the "réseau" "semé de larmes" betokened the extinction of this beautiful Art.

The peculiarity by which Point d'Alençon can always be recognised is its "cordonnet," which is firmer and clearer than that of any other Lace, owing, it is said, to the fact that it is worked over horsehair; it is also firmly and closely covered with button-hole stitching throughout. The Alençon "réseau" is shown in Fig. 3, Illustration I. It is made with a double-twisted thread throughout, the looped stitches being twisted on to horizontal threads previously fixed across the width of the Lace, giving an effect of lines or rows to the network.

Point d'Alençon is Lace of a very fine order, both from the beauty of the designs during the time of its prime, and also from the wonderful delicacy of its workmanship, which last can scarcely be appreciated except with the help of a magnifying glass. The specimen shown in Illustration XXI. is part of a lappet, the length of which is divided into sections by a very beautiful framework filled in with delicate "à jours"; each section contains a little group representing one of La Fontaine's fables; a truly marvellous triumph of needlework.

Illustration XXVII.

Chantilly.

Point d'Argentan

Argentan is a town in the immediate neighbourhood of Alençon, and the Lace was made there under the same direction. Its marked peculiarity is that the "réseau" ground is not made of single threads only, but that the sides of each mesh are worked over with button-hole stitch. (See Fig. 4, Illustration I.) The work is so fine that it can scarcely be detected with the naked eye, but the effect can easily be recognised as the hexagonal mesh is larger, and has a stiffer appearance, than is the case with any other Needle-made lace.

Valenciennes Pillow Lace

This most beautiful of French Pillow laces is now no longer made in France itself, its manufacture having been transferred to Ypres, in Belgium.

It belongs to that class of Pillow lace which is made in one piece on the pillow, the same threads forming both "toilé" and "réseau" alike.

The peculiarity of all Valenciennes Lace is the absence of any "cordonnet"; also the closeness and evenness of the texture of the "toilé" which resembles the finest cambric; but notwithstanding that these characteristics may always be recognised, there is a very great difference between the earlier and the later styles of the Lace. In the preceding pages it has been explained that the earliest Pillow lace was not made with the "réseau" ground; on the contrary, this was one of the latest developments of the lace-making Art. Even when "bride" work had been abandoned there occurred a transition state before the simple net-like character of the "réseau" was perfected, and accordingly we find the earliest Valenciennes Lace grounded with, so to speak, a fancy mesh, thicker and closer in effect than the open "réseau" of later date. The difference will be seen between the two specimens shown in Illustration XXIV., and there also will be seen a difference in the style of design strongly corroborative of the above statement; for the specimen given of the thick-grounded Lace is in excellent Renaissance style, whereas the later Lace has degenerated into naturalistic floral representation. It would appear that the early Valenciennes Lace was produced, generally, in the neighbouring district, but that it was in the town itself that the pure "réseau" was invented, and forthwith the town workers, proud of their invention, proceeded to appropriate to their Lace the name of "Vraie Valenciennes," pretending that this Lace could not be made elsewhere; and they moreover stigmatised the older style still produced in the country villages as "Fausse Valenciennes." The palm of merit would not be now altogether awarded in their sense; notice the beautiful specimen shown in Illustration XXV. Here a Renaissance framework encloses a naturalistically treated carnation flower. The carnation has ever been a favourite with embroiderers and lace-workers, and in this instance is most beautifully represented.

The "réseau" of the "Vraie Valenciennes" is made of four threads plaited throughout (see Fig. 7, Illustration II.), hence its great durability and the name given to it by its admirers, "Les éternelles Valenciennes."

Point de Paris

It is sometimes contended that there is no special Lace properly called by this name, but that it is merely the designation of a particular kind of "réseau," also described as the Fond Chant "réseau." (See Fig. 8, Illustration II.) Still there is no doubt that a manufacture of some sort of simple Lace was carried on extensively during the seventeenth and eighteenth centuries, in the Isle de France and in Paris itself, until annihilated by the Revolution, and that its characteristic was this same "réseau." As shown in the specimen—Illustration XXVI.—the style of pattern is extremely simple, and consists usually of small leafy sprays, united to form a straight edge with "picots."

The industry is believed to have been first founded by Huguenots, and encouraged by Henry IV. and Sully, but no Lace of great artistic pretension was ever produced.

Lille

Lille has been a French town since the treaty of Aix-la-Chapelle in 1668; its productions should therefore be properly included among French Laces, though in character they are more nearly akin to those of Flanders.

In appearance there is indeed a strong resemblance to Mechlin; the special difference between the two is in the character of the "réseau." That of Lille Lace is known as "Fond simple" or "Fond clair." It is made of two threads only, and these simply crossed, not

Illustration XXVIII.

Blonde.

plaited, at their junction (see Fig. 6, Illustration II.); by this peculiarity Lille Lace can be always recognised. The pattern is outlined with a "cordonnet" of flat untwisted coarse thread. The edge of the Lace is usually quite straight, not scolloped or wavy, and oval openings are left in the pattern near the edge and filled with ornamental "à jours." The "réseau" is often sprinkled with small square dots.

Chantilly

Though the silk Lace of France is mostly known under this name, yet its manufacture was extensively carried on at Caen, Bayeux, and Le Puy, as well as at Chantilly.

It is made both in black and white silk, and its distinguishing peculiarity is the use of the six-pointed star "réseau," the "Point de Paris" already mentioned, also known by the name of "Fond Chant," an abbreviation of Chantilly. (See Fig. 8, Illustration II.) It is generally used in conjunction with the "Fond simple" of Lille. The pattern of Chantilly Lace is outlined with a "cordonnet" of a flat untwisted silk strand.

BLONDE,

also made in the same districts, has a "réseau" of the Lille type made of fine twisted silk, while the "toilé" is worked entirely with a broad flat strand, producing a very attractive glistening effect. The name "Blonde" originated from the use of écru instead of bleached silk, hence "blonde" or flaxen.

The manufacture of silk Lace at Chantilly and in the neighbourhood was established in the seventeenth century by the Duchesse de Longueville, and owing to her patronage and also probably to the vicinity of Paris it became for a time very popular. At the Revolution the demand for it, of course, at once ceased, and not only so, but being looked upon as royal *protégés* the unfortunate lace-makers were involved in the ruin of their patrons, and most of them perished by the guillotine. During the Empire, however, Chantilly and also Blonde came again into fashion, and since that time the demand for black silk Blonde for Spanish mantillas alone, has kept up the prosperity of the trade, which, however, is by no means confined to any one town, but flourishes throughout the province of Calvados.

OF OTHER FRENCH PILLOW LACES

Normandy, during the seventeenth and eighteenth centuries, was a very important district for Pillow lace-making in France, Valenciennes at the time forming part of Flanders.

The picturesque head-dresses of the peasant women no doubt encouraged the manufacture. In 1692, in Dieppe alone, four thousand women were employed in lace-making, and at Havre, Honfleur, Bolbec, Eu, and Fécamps the trade was also in a very flourishing condition. The Lace produced was of a simple character, much resembling the modern Valenciennes edgings; it is often mentioned in inventories and letters of the day as being used by the upper classes, especially as trimmings for under-linen. But the Revolution passed over this district as elsewhere like a destroying blight, and the lace-making trade was for a time utterly extinguished. In 1826 some nuns attempted to revive the manufacture, and a Lace school was started at Dieppe with some success. The kind of Lace is, however, unfortunately of all others the easiest to imitate by machinery; indeed, only workers themselves, it has been said, can detect the very slight difference that exists between ordinary Valenciennes edging, as made on the pillow, and the best that is produced by the loom. Under these circumstances, as purchasers will naturally always gravitate to the cheapest market, it is no wonder if hand-work, of necessity more laborious, and consequently more costly, cannot be made remunerative.

Of Flemish Laces

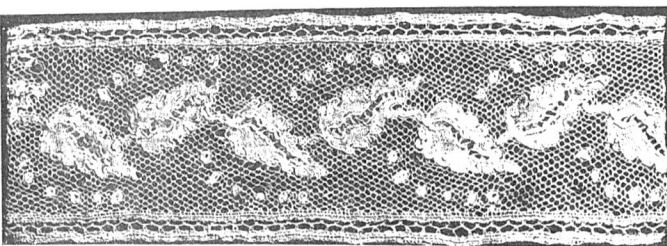

Mechlin.

Reversing what we have seen to be the case with Italian Lace, the earliest Flemish Lace was undoubtedly made on the pillow, though as to whether the Art originated in Flanders or was imported from Venice, there is great difference of opinion. The arguments on both sides have been stated earlier. But some further light seems to be thrown on the subject, when the character of the early Flemish Lace is observed. According to the opinion of most writers, borne out by the chronological arrangement of the catalogue of the South Kensington Museum, the earliest Lace made in Flanders was of the kind known as Pillow Guipure. The pattern is made as of tape in a flowing Renaissance style, sometimes connected by "brides," sometimes altogether without "brides," when the points of the pattern touch each other.

There are many specimens of this Lace in the Museum so nearly like Italian Lace of the same kind, that the description there given of them is "Flemish or Italian." Two specimens are here shown in Illustration XXIX. of this Lace, and in these specimens at any rate a distinction can be observed which seems to mark them as Flemish. The thread used is much finer, and at the same time the work is looser and less firm than that seen in acknowledged Italian Pillow lace. However that may be, no one accustomed to Italian design can look at them without feeling sure that the inspiration of such Lace was certainly that of the Italian Renaissance, even though produced in Flanders, and if so, then the natural conclusion will be that such Pillow lace was in its origin Italian.

Thus much has been said, in order that the student may not be perplexed when finding Lace of undoubted Italian character attributed with good evidence to Belgium.

In Flanders, as elsewhere, Pillow lace "à brides" was antecedent to that made with the "réseau" ground. In specimen Fig. 1 one can almost see how the one was developed out of the other. The pattern was too loose to admit of large open spaces, and as it was easier

Illustration XXIX.

Flemish Pillow Lace (two specimens).

held together by many ties than by few, these interlaced, and fell into regular arrangement, foreshadowing the mesh of the future "réseau."

The exact time at which this was fully developed seems uncertain. Portraiture in England, at least in this case, is of little or no assistance, owing to the vicious taste of the day which induced Sir Peter Lely and others to represent their sitters as draped in loose floating masses of blue or white satin, arranged in a supposed classical but impossible manner, and fastened on the thigh or the shoulder with an equally impossible jewel. But fortunately Art in Holland was less imaginative; and in a portrait of Fräulein Verbiest, by Gonzales Coqués, we see Lace with a "réseau" ground very clearly depicted. Coqués died in 1684; the invention therefore must have been anterior to that date.

Mr. Alan Cole, whose short introduction to the catalogue of Lace in the South Kensington Museum is an admirably clear exposition of the subject, is of opinion that "the origin of 'réseau' grounds may be considered to lie first in the use of the net ground for 'Lacis' or Darned netting, the 'Punto a maglia quadra,' for which Vinciolo made many designs" (the pattern books alluded to in a preceding chapter). "He was in the employment of the French Court towards the end of the sixteenth century, and at this time the early form of Pillow lace was being produced, and as it proceeded and became more and more developed, the making of meshes in small series of twos and threes also developed" (see Fig. I, Illustration XXIX.) "and expanded into larger spaces filled with 'réseau.' It seems likely that this development was stimulated by the contemporary production of the Darned net-work, which the lace-workers would be ambitious of reproducing on the pillow."

The earliest "réseau" grounded Lace made in Flanders had a large irregular mesh, and was called "Fond de brides."

Brussels Pillow Lace

This has, all along, retained a trace of its origin from Pillow Guipure, in that like its Genoese original, and *unlike other Flemish Laces*, it is not made in one piece on the pillow, but the pattern is first made by itself, and the "réseau" ground is worked in round it afterwards. The peculiarity is easily recognised; for in consequence of the way in which it is worked, the long threads that form the "toilé" of Brussels Lace of *all dates* always follow the curves of the pattern, whereas with other Flemish Laces in which pattern and "réseau" are made together in one piece on the pillow, however varied the forms may be, these threads are found to run parallel to the edge of the whole length of the Lace, and to pass across through the pattern into the "réseau" ground. (See diagram.)

Brussels.   Mechlin.

Here we have the first peculiarity by which Brussels Pillow lace can be recognised. Secondly, it is to be noticed that the "réseau" of Brussels Lace, as seen through a magnifying glass, has a hexagonal mesh, of which two sides are made of four threads plaited four times, and four sides of two threads twisted twice. (See Fig. 3, Illustration II.) Thirdly, Brussels Pillow lace has two sorts of "toilé"; one, the usual woven texture as of a piece of cambric; the other a more open arrangement of the threads, having very much the appearance of the Fond Chant "réseau." (See Fig. 2, Illustration II.) This is used with great effect to represent shading in the production of flower forms, especially in modern Lace. Fourthly, the pattern of Brussels Lace is not outlined with a "cordonnet," but a little line of openwork stitches forms the edge instead. (See diagram.) Brussels Pillow lace is also distinguished by the beauty of its designs, more freedom being possible in consequence of the manner in which it was worked.

The extreme fineness of the thread in old Brussels Pillow lace is also to be noticed. It was spun, we are told, in dark, damp cellars, where only one ray of light was arranged to fall on the thread, which was otherwise almost invisible; also because in a drier air it would have been too brittle. But such hand-spun thread is now too costly for use, and machine-made thread is always substituted.

Although the characteristics enumerated above may always be recognised, yet the Brussels Pillow lace of to-day bears but slight resemblance to the manufactures of the seventeenth century. It has gone through many styles in pattern and make, which may be classed as follows:—

Point d'Angleterre

On the first invention of the perfectly formed "réseau" ground, about the middle of the seventeenth century, this was worked on the pillow in the following manner: threads were hooked on to the little open edge of the "toilé" of the pattern, and with these the "réseau" was worked in round the pattern to fill up the ground. "Réseau" made in this manner is called the "vrai réseau," and Brussels Lace thus worked is properly styled "Point d'Angleterre." The specimen shown in Illustration XXX. of this early style has a characteristic peculiarity, namely, the raised rib of plaited threads marking the veins of the leaves and outlining the salient parts.

It is interesting to compare this specimen with the early Valenciennes lappet shown in Illustration XXV.; though the method of execution is radically different the design is almost identical, showing the interchange of patterns which took place between various contemporary Lace manufactories. It is a lesson that one cannot altogether trust to the style of the pattern in judging of the local character of Lace.

"Point d'Angleterre" was also often made with open spaces left either round the pattern or in diagonal bars, and these were filled in with pillow-made "brides picotées." This Lace is called "Point d'Angleterre à brides." A very beautiful example is given in Illustration XXXI., which is further interesting on account of the fine Needle-point fillings that have been superadded. When such is the case the Lace is called "mixed Lace."

Many explanations have been given for the use of the name "Point d'Angleterre," for a Lace that is neither Point nor made in England. M. Seguin favours the theory that the Lace was of English origin, and that it was only subsequently produced in Brussels; but there seems to be but little ground for that view. The opinion more usually held is that when, about the year 1660, its importation into England, as well as into France, was forbidden by prohibitive duties, the Lace merchants nevertheless found means to smuggle it across by sea to English ports and then sold it here, and exported, it into France as "Point d'Angleterre." To this day all Brussels Lace is indiscriminately so called in France.

The ladies of Louis the Fifteenth's Court, in the days when hoops and powder were in fashion, particularly affected this Lace. In England the protective duties were removed in 1699, and here too, during the reigns of George the First and George the Second, in spite

Illustration XXX.

Old Brussels Pillow Lace—"Point d'Anglaterre"

of great efforts made to encourage native lace-making, ruffles, lappets, and flounces were most admired when made of Brussels Lace. Such Lace at this time was made in pieces of considerable size, and in this case the "réseau" was worked in narrow strips from an inch and a half to two inches wide, and afterwards joined together to the required width with the needle, but so skilfully as almost to elude detection.

Brussels Lace, "à vrai réseau," continued to be produced until the catastrophe of the French Revolution, which had its effect upon this as upon all other centres of the Lace industry; but here, it was not the only cause of the decline of the Art. The invention of machine-made net had been perfected in Nottingham about the year 1810, and from that time forward the Brussels lace-workers adopted the plan of appliquéing their Pillow-made patterns on this comparatively inexpensive material, and the "vrai réseau" worked on the pillow is now never made except by special order for Royalty or for exhibition purposes.

Lace so appliquéd can be distinguished from that made with the "vrai réseau" by the fact that the net ground, though sometimes cut away, is often seen to pass behind the lace pattern, and also by the character of the network; machine-made net is composed of diamond-shaped meshes, and is made with two threads only, very tightly twisted and crossed, not plaited, at their junction, and is quite unlike the Brussels pillow "réseau" shown in Fig. 3, Illustration II.

Brussels Pillow Lace appliquéd on machine-made net is known as "Point plat appliqué." The term "Plat" is used to distinguish it from Needle-point Brussels, also sometimes appliqué. The innovation described above was very fatal to the character of Brussels Lace. The designs grew more and more attenuated and detached as the temptation was felt to spread the pattern more sparsely over the net ground. Owing to the naturalistic taste of the day also, the finely composed conventional ornament of an earlier date was abandoned in favour of representations of natural flowers. A still later but better style of Brussels Lace is the

Point Duchesse.

In this the pattern is grounded entirely with Pillow-made "brides," and the "réseau" is altogether absent. The designs are necessarily more continuous than in the preceding Lace, and they are often very good.

The name of this Lace is of comparatively recent date, but the style itself existed earlier, under the designation of "Guipure façon Angleterre."

Brussels Needle-Point Lace

Brussels is the only Flemish centre for the manufacture of Needle-point lace.

In Flanders lace-making started from the invention or adoption of Pillow lace, and it seems evident that it was only in consequence of a spirit of emulation, and of the example set by the French lace-workers of Alençon, that needle lace-making was started at Brussels, about the year 1720. A proof of its late adoption is, that Brussels Needle-point was never made with "brides" only, as we have seen was the case with the early Needle-points of Venice, and also with the work first produced in France.

It is interesting here to note how the influence of neighbouring countries and districts acted and reacted on each other. The Needle-point "réseau" of Alençon was practically a copy, with the needle, of the pillow ground of Flanders, and now in turn Flemish workers borrowed, or more probably stole, from France the secrets of Needle lace, including the invention originally copied from themselves.

The earliest Brussels Point very nearly resembles that of Alençon. The work is generally, however, not quite so close and firm, and the "toilé" is looser and flatter. The "cordonnet," instead of being entirely covered with button-hole stitches, as is the case with Alençon Lace, is left in an unfinished state as a strand of threads. There is also a difference in the "réseau"; in Brussels Lace it is made with a simple looped stitch, whereas in the Alençon "réseau" the loops are whipped over at their base with an additional thread. (See Figs. 2, 3, Illustration I.) This peculiarity has been continued to the present day, the "réseau" of modern "Point de Gaze" being so worked.

Illustration XXXI.

"Point d'Angleterre à brides."

The style of the designs of Brussels Point is rarely of so fine a Renaissance type as in the best French Lace. The patterns are usually such as were also worked at the time on the pillow; but where patterns as well as inventions were so frequently interchanged, it is impossible to draw any certain distinction from such differences. The uncovered "cordonnet" and the simply looped "réseau" are the safest indications.

The earliest Brussels Needle-point was grounded with a needle "réseau," but examples of such Lace are not very common. The Brussels lace-makers were justly celebrated for their beautiful Pillow-made "réseau," and being more familiar with its practice they seem to have preferred to use it. Thus we find much of their best Needle lace grounded with the "vrai réseau" worked on the pillow, in the same way as with the "Point d'Angleterre"; this is the case with the specimen shown in Fig. 1, Illustration XXXIII.

Illustration XXXII.

Modern Brussels.
1. Point Duchesse.   2. Point Plat Appliqué.

At the beginning of this century Brussels Needle lace underwent the same process of decline, and from the same causes that we have seen to have affected the Pillow lace; it degenerated into—

Point Appliqué,

that is, the Needle lace pattern instead of being grounded with the "vrai réseau," was appliquéd on to machine-made net; and as the demand for a less expensive style of work grew greater at the same time that labour became dearer, the patterns became more and more slender and were more thinly scattered over the ground. In Illustration XXXIII. two specimens are shown. Fig. 1 represents a piece of early Brussels Point grounded with the

Pillow-made "vrai réseau," and Fig. 2 a late piece of "Point Appliqué." If for no other reason, this later style is to be deprecated on account of the quality of the net, which is always partly, often entirely, made of cotton; it shrinks the first time it is washed, causing the curves of the needle-worked pattern to become crumpled and shapeless, and if, in order to avoid this misfortune, the Lace is sent to Brussels to be cleaned, it is, we understand, only possible to do so by dipping it in white lead, with the certain result that the whole will in time turn the colour of rust.

Point De Gaze

It is a pleasure to record that of late years an honest return has been made by the Brussels lace- workers to early Needle-point traditions. The beautiful modern Lace known as "Point de Gaze" is made entirely with the needle, and is grounded with its own "réseau." Partly to suit modern taste in design, and partly perhaps from economy of work when labour is so dear, the execution is much more open and slight than in the early Lace, but this very slightness is skilfully made use of to produce an extremely elegant effect; part of the "toilé" is made in close and part in open stitch, giving an appearance of shading, and the open parts are very prettily enriched with dotting. If to those who delight in the soft richness of the work of former times the execution of the "Point de Gaze" seems somewhat thin and loose, and the style of the patterns rather too naturalistic, it must be allowed that to many, the result produced is a certain lightness and delicacy to which the old Brussels Point did not attain; and one must be glad that when an almost unlimited demand for cheaper goods is in every direction flooding the market and pressing down the price at which Lace can be sold, the Brussels craftsmen should have taken up again their old Art and have been able to produce so beautiful a fabric.

Of Flemish Lace

The best known Flemish Laces, other than Brussels, are: Mechlin, Binche, Ypres, and Antwerp. All these belong to that class of Pillow lace which is made in one piece on the pillow, the same threads passing across the whole width of the Lace and forming both the ground and the pattern.

Mechlin (Fr. Malines).

All Flemish Lace was at one time classed under this name, but the earliest that can be distinctively so called was made with a "réseau" ground about the year 1720. The special characteristics of Mechlin Lace are: first, the "cordonnet" of a flat silky thread which always outlines the pattern; and, secondly, the hexagonal mesh of the "réseau." It is made of two threads twisted twice on four sides, and four threads plaited three times on the two other sides; thus the plait is shorter, and the mesh consequently smaller than that of Brussels Lace. (See Illustration II., Figs. 3, 4.) This Lace is sometimes grounded with an ornamental "réseau," instead of one in the usual hexagonal shape, called "Fond de neige" or "Œil de perdrix," and also occasionally with the six-pointed "Fond Chant," but these varieties are not common.

Illustration XXXIII.

1. Old Brussels Needle-point.   2. Modern Brussels Needle-point Appliqué.

In the earliest Mechlin Lace the style of designs very much resembles that of Brussels, though rather heavier and less graceful; it is needless to repeat, however, that though the patterns may be alike, the totally different method of construction always marks the difference between the two.

The quatrefoil flower pattern seen in Illustration XXXV., as a filling to the spaces of the conventional scroll-work, is very characteristic of this period.

Illustration XXXVI. shows another imitation of Brussels designs. In this specimen of "Malines à brides" the peculiarities of "Point d'Angleterre" are very closely followed, even to the open spaces filled in with "bride"-like "à jours."

But Mechlin, when at the height of its popularity, had evolved a style of its own. The pattern, more or less floral, always formed the edge of the Lace, and the "réseau" ground

Illustration XXXIV.

Modern Brussels Needle-point— "Point de Gaze"

was sprinkled with small flowers or spots. The rose and the carnation, two very favourite flowers with lace-makers, were represented with singular fidelity. The Lace of this period is perhaps one of the prettiest in existence. It is so light and soft, the pattern and the "réseau" are so well balanced, and the designs so graceful, that it well deserves its title of the Queen of Laces. The fine Indian muslins which became the fashion at the court of Marie Antoinette could support no heavier ornament, and accordingly we see it abundantly introduced in the portraits of the day.

In England it has been always a favourite, and few are the collections of old family Lace in which some beautiful specimens are not to be found.

But this Lace, like all others, had its day of decline in. taste as well as in popularity. The French Revolution was a blow severely felt, and when the lace trade revived under the Empire, perhaps the old patterns had been lost or forgotten, or were found too expensive for sale, and so a thinner and more meagre style of design was adopted. But the revival was not long-lived, and now the manufacture is altogether discontinued.

Binche

Lace of a very fine and delicate description is attributed to this town.

Its characteristics are, that there is either no "cordonnet" at all outlining the pattern, or that the "cordonnet" is scarcely a thicker thread than that which-makes the "toilé." The ground can scarcely be called a "réseau," for there are no meshes, but instead, a spider's-web-like material, closely sprinkled with small round spots or discs. It is called a "Fond de neige," and in truth really resembles snowflakes. A fanciful author has described it as a Dutch garden of flowers covered with snow.

Illustration XXXV.

Early Mechlin.

This is one of the earliest of Flemish Laces, as is shown by the absence of any regular "réseau." The kind of work has now been quite given up, and Mrs. Palliser says that the lace-makers of Binche in her time employed themselves in making the sprigs for Brussels Point plat appliqué.

On the same illustration is shown a specimen of so-called Trolle Kant; Kant being the Flemish word for Lace, and Trolle, to judge from the use of the corresponding word "Trolly" in Buckinghamshire, signifying the coarse outlining "cordonnet." The specimen is interesting as being a rough representation of the general style of early Flemish designs.

Ypres

As has been said, the manufacture of Valenciennes Lace, which has entirely disappeared from the place of its birth, has been continued at Ypres and in the neighbourhood. The Lace is made in exactly the same manner as was formerly the "Vraie Valenciennes," but it is inferior in workmanship, and in variety and beauty of design. Its character is too well known to require description; it need only be said here that like the old Valenciennes, the pattern is not outlined with any "cordonnet," and that the "réseau" is made with a plait of four threads, and forms a diamond-shaped mesh.

Antwerp

The best known Lace made at Antwerp is the so-called "Potten Kant," or Pot lace, from the representation of a pot or vase of flowers with which it is always decorated.

Illustration XXXVI.

1. Early Mechlin (à brides).   2. Later Mechlin (à brides).

Some have considered this pattern to be a survival from an earlier design, including the figure of the Virgin and the Annunciation, though it does not seem certain that any such larger composition has ever been seen. The pot varies very much in size and details. The accompanying illustration shows a very handsome one, with some exceedingly well-represented carnation flowers; but, large or small, no Antwerp woman's cap was in former days considered properly trimmed without this ornament. The Lace is usually grounded with a coarse "Fond Chant."

In various places in Flanders, besides those above mentioned, many kinds of Lace, more or less coarse, have been made, but without any such special distinction as to require separate notice; they can be usually recognised as Flemish by a resemblance to the characteristics already described, as those of the more important manufactures.

POINT AND PILLOW LACE

Illustration XXXVII.

1. Binche.   2. Flemish "Trolle Kant."

Illustration XXXVIII.

Antwerp "Potten Kant."

Of English and Irish Lace

Limerick Lace.

Linen Cut-work was made in England very extensively during the sixteenth century. It was a favourite accomplishment of the ladies of Queen Elizabeth's time, and it supplied, moreover, a profitable occupation for a large class of professional workwomen. There was an enormous demand for Lace of the finer sort for ruffs, and the thicker linen Lace was largely used to trim sheets and table linen, etc. We see it represented on the cradle monument to the infant daughter of James the First in Westminster Abbey, and also on the dress of her elder sister, whose recumbent figure in effigy lies hard by. An actual relic of the kind, possessing a peculiar interest, is to be found to this day in a cottage in the village of Shottery, in Warwickshire, which is still occupied by descendants of the family of Anne Hathaway, Shakespeare's wife. On an old oak bedstead in an upstairs room there is displayed the best linen sheet which, as tradition says, was kept for special family occasions, such as births, christenings, weddings, funerals, etc. It has a narrow strip, about an inch and a half wide, of Cut-work made in the linen, and joining two breadths together where there would otherwise be a seam. The pattern is of a very simple zigzag character. The bolster cover, now kept in a frame, has a rather wider band of a more ambitious design, but of the same style of work. There seems every reason to believe that this relic is authentic, and as it might very well date from Elizabethan times, it is possible that our great poet himself may have seen or even used this bed furniture in the house of his wife's parents.

Besides articles for use, domestic or otherwise, a considerable number of samplers have come down to us. They were worked at schools or kept as collections of patterns of

Illustration XXXIX.

English Cut-work.

embroidery by industrious housewives. Illustration XXXIX. represents part of one in the collection of the South Kensington Museum, with two patterns of Cut-work, rather clumsy and heavy in style, but, as will be seen, worked in the usual Italian manner. (See Illus. I., Fig. 5.) Bands of embroidery patterns of various kinds other than Cut-work fill up a strip of linen of about a yard and a half long. It is signed and dated "Elizabeth Mackett 1696." But beyond Cut-work, no great amount of Needle lace seems ever to have been made in England. Bone lace (that is, Pillow lace) is constantly alluded to in Queen Elizabeth's wardrobe accounts, and though a good deal no doubt came from Flanders and Genoa, there is evidence to show that by the beginning of the seventeenth century the native lace-making trade was in a flourishing condition in many parts of England.

Its chief centres have always been in Devonshire (especially Honiton), Bedfordshire, and Buckinghamshire.

Honiton Lace

It has been mentioned in connection with the name "Point d'Angleterre" that the theory is sometimes entertained that this Lace originated in England, and was only afterwards transferred to Brussels. The probability, however, seems to be that, on the contrary, the

Art came to England from Flanders, as some have supposed in consequence of an immigration of Protestants during a time of persecution. However that may be, Mrs. Treadwin mentions in her valuable book on *Antique Point and Honiton*, that Pillow lace of some sort was made in this district some time before the year 1617. It was probably not at all like that now produced in Devonshire, but rather a sort of open woven braid with a simple diamond-shaped lozenge pattern of a kind still sometimes to be met with. Our present use of the word Lace in "bootlaces," etc., may be a clue to what was called Lace in early English times—namely, a plaited braid, more or less ornamental.

During the troubles of the Civil War and the Commonwealth ornament in dress was naturally in abeyance, but on the return of the Court in 1660 Lace also resumed its place in society. It was, however, speedily confronted with difficulties of a fiscal nature, when, in order to increase the revenue and also perhaps to protect native trade, prohibitive duties were put upon its importation from abroad. We have seen in a previous chapter how these were evaded; it was doubtless, however, at this time, and in consequence of these duties, that Flemish lace-workers must have been induced to come over to England to teach their art in Devonshire. The absolute identity in the method of working Honiton and Brussels Lace can scarcely otherwise be accounted for.

Early Devonshire Lace appears, however, sometimes to have had one peculiarity distinguishing it both from Brussels and from the later Honiton. It is the use of an outlining "cordonnet" or trolly or gimp, from which it was locally known as Trolly lace.

The development of this Lace has followed much the same course as did those of Flanders. As with Brussels "Point d'Angleterre," the pattern part of Honiton having been made first on the pillow by itself, the "réseau" in early times was worked in round it, also on the pillow; but later, after the invention of machine-made net, the principle of "appliqué" work was also adopted in England, and this cheaper and inferior material was substituted for the hand-made ground.

The difference between Honiton and Brussels Pillow lace is one of quality rather than of kind. English designs have been as a rule less artistic than those in use in Brussels.

Even in the best specimens produced during the early part of this century garlands and bouquets of natural flowers have been put together without much idea or knowledge of composition. The execution, also, was in general less finished and delicate than in good Brussels Lace. But these remarks apply rather to the past; of late years schools of Design and the emulation excited by International Exhibitions have much improved the character of English Lace on both points. The difference between the two specimens shown in Illustration XL. will be at once noticed. No. 1 represents Lace made in the early half of this century. The flower sprigs are rather thick and heavy in shape and are "appliquéd" on to machine-made net. No. 2 shows a recent production. The pattern is bold and continuous as well as graceful, and the ground is a very good needle-worked "réseau"—it is a mixed Lace, in fact. Much of the best Honiton now made is in this style. A "Duchesse" lace, very similar to that made in Brussels (see Illustration XXXII.), is also now worked in Devonshire.

Illustration XL.

1. Honiton Appliqué. 2. Honiton Appliqué with needle "réseau" ground.

BUCKINGHAMSHIRE AND BEDFORDSHIRE LACE

There is a tradition that while Catherine of Aragon, the forsaken Queen of Henry the Eighth, was living at Ampthill Park, in Bedfordshire, about 1532, waiting with what patience she might for the decision of the Pope respecting her divorce, she beguiled her sadness by exercising her own skill in needlework and required the ladies of her household to do the same. Not only so, but she interested herself in teaching lace-making to the village women of the district, and this was the origin of the Bedfordshire lace industry. To confirm the truth of the story, it is said that till well within the present century the name-day of the kind but most unhappy lady, St. Catherine's Day, the 25th November, was annually kept as a treat-day for young lace-makers, and children expected a feast of cakes

1. Buckinghamshire Baby Lace.   2. Buckinghamshire Spider Pattern.

and sweets, and called the day "Kattern's Day." St. Catherine is also the patron saint of girls and unmarried women. But the Lace then taught by the Spanish princess to the Bedfordshire women was certainly not anything like the present Pillow lace; more probably it was Cut-work or Reticella made out of linen, an Art which we know to have been practised in Italy and Spain at the time, and which there is the early evidence of old English samplers to prove was also, though with less taste, made in England.

Some thirty years after Queen Catherine's death another impetus was given to the lace industry by the arrival in the neighbourhood of certain Flemish lace-workers, who had fled from the persecutions of the Duke of Alva, and settled in the south midland counties. These introduced a kind of Pillow lace known by the name of "Bone lace."

The earliest mention of Lace under this name is in 1554, when it is said to have trimmed the dress worn by Sir Thomas Wyatt at his execution; in the accounts of Queen Elizabeth's wardrobe the name is of constant recurrence.

After the revocation of the Edict of Nantes, in 1685, another immigration of foreign lace-makers took place, this time from the French provinces bordering on Flanders, and it is doubtless to these last that the distinctly Flemish character of the old Bedfordshire and Buckinghamshire Lace is to be attributed.

Again, in 1794 it is recorded in the *Annual Register* that "a number of engenuous french emigrants have found employment in the manufacture of Lace" in these counties. Thus it would seem as though one foreign settlement attracted another.

The Lace of the two counties may be classed together as being practically the same. They belong to that class of Lace which is worked in one piece on the pillow, and in their general character and style of design they strongly resemble the Lace manufactured at Lille. The "réseau" ground is exactly the same as that of Lille Lace, that is, it is composed of two threads twisted and simply crossed, not plaited, at their junction. The mesh varies a little in shape, from a four-sided diamond shape to a hexagon, according as the threads at crossing are drawn tighter or left loose and long. Like Lille, the pattern of Buckinghamshire Lace is outlined with a coarse silky thread, called locally the "Trolly," from the Flemish word "Trolle."

The style of designs, also, of the English Lace has been clearly influenced by Lille models. There are often the same oval-shaped openings filled with various fancy "à jours." In No. 2, Illustration XLI., a specimen is shown which goes by the name of "Spider lace," on account of the open-work filling. No. 1 represents what is called "Baby lace," a variety with a finer "réseau" and smaller pattern, made on purpose for trimming baby-linen; and here again, by the small square dots on the ground, one is reminded of a frequent peculiarity in Lille Lace.

From the time of the first Flemish settlement till almost the middle of the present century, the lace industry gave constant occupation to many hundreds of women and children in the district. Its chief centres were at Great Marlow, Olney, Stony Stratford, Newport Pagnel, and High Wycombe; but these towns were probably only where the Lace was collected from the workers, to be sold by middle-men, the work itself being carried on in most of the country villages. It was still then called Bone lace; the origin of the term is not easy to ascertain. Several explanations have been given—that the little bones of sheeps' trotters were at first used as bobbins; that till the brass pins used in lace-making for fixing the work in its place became cheap enough to be general, fishbones were substituted; also that the patterns were pricked out on thin plates of bone instead of on the parchment in later use. The fact that the Lace has also been called "Parchment lace" gives a colour to this last theory.

Old bobbins are often found made of bone instead of wood. They are sometimes very curiously decorated, indeed they seem to have been often used as love-tokens between the young people of the day. They are to be seen stained with red or other colours, and ingeniously turned in ribs or stripes; rings of metal are fastened to them at intervals, or brass wire is wound round them, and "gingles" or bunches of coloured beads are hung from the end strung on a loop of wire, these last being also of use in increasing the tension of the thread by adding to the weight of the bobbin; and, lastly, mottoes of various kinds are, so to speak, tattooed on them, the letters being outlined by pricked holes filled with colour. Sometimes it is the name of the giver, as "dear Joseph," which is so inscribed; sometimes the girl's name, as "Sarah"; and sometimes a three-lined motto, as—

Illustration XLII.

An Old Lace Chest.

"Love Me Or
  Leave Me A
    Lone For Ever."

Not only the bobbins, but the pillow also was the subject of much pride and pleasure, and even the pins were objects of ornamentation. Children gathered the little prickly seeds of the hedgerow Bed-straw (*Galium*) and threaded them on the pins, which, when dry, formed little brown heads as hard, and much the same colour as if made of walnut wood.

An illustration of some ornamented bobbins and also of a Lace token will be found at the end of this chapter. The latter were used by employers of labour as payment to their work-people at the end of the last century, when the country seems to have suffered from a scarcity of mint-coined money. They were issued as country bank-notes are now, and were redeemable at a fixed rate when presented to the central office.

The old oak chest shown above is another relic of the prosperous days of lace-making in Buckinghamshire. The upper part was intended to hold the lace pillow, while the drawers below were to take the bobbins and patterns.

It was shortly after the beginning of this century, however, that Machine lace was invented and became generally known, and thenceforward the hand-made Lace trade had but a precarious existence. In order to keep the favour of the purchasing public, continual changes have been made in the style of the Lace produced. Silk Lace called "Blonde"—because being made with raw silk it was "fair," not white in colour—was one of the earliest new introductions; to that succeeded Maltese and the so-called "Cluny," named after no place of its manufacture, but from the Museum of Antiquities in the Hotel Cluny in Paris, and because the Lace was supposed to have a mediaeval appearance. It is a plaited Lace, somewhat resembling the Genoese and Maltese Laces, and is made both in black silk and in white cotton. And here, alas! is the secret of the inferiority, and much of the want of success of this modern English Lace; it is almost always made of cotton, and not linen thread, the probable reason being that the material is more within the means of the cottage workers. After Cluny came coloured worsted Lace and Torchon lace, and this is now the kind mostly produced. Besides, however, the competition of steam machinery, and the consequent lowering of prices, another enemy has lately come into the field against the Buckinghamshire lace-workers, in the shape of the Board of Education. Children in former times began to learn to use their bobbins at five years old, and at twelve were able to support themselves entirely by their work, and it is said, with some show of reason, that unless the Art is so acquired by the workers when very young, there is but small likelihood that sufficient skill will ever be attained to make it remunerative at the low prices for which alone Lace can be sold. But the inspector insists that the children shall be sent to school, and such short time as is allowed for school instruction in work is not spent in teaching lace-making. So it comes to pass that the young girls of this generation have not learnt the work properly, and do not care to practise it; and the Lace that is made now, and for which a market is anxiously sought, is made by the old women of a former generation between sixty and seventy years old and more. And when in a few years time they must have passed away, it is to be feared that the Art of lace-making, in this district at any rate, will have disappeared also with them.

Great efforts have been and are still being made, however, to save this national Art from extinction. Exhibitions are organised, and prizes offered for the best work by such gentry of the district as are kindly disposed towards their poorer neighbours, and whatever may be the results of these efforts, much sympathy must be felt for their object. For, apart from the fact that one must regret to see the disappearance of any of our old English handicrafts, this one, as we have seen, has in former times been a source of great interest and pride, as well as of income, to the poor cottage women, who otherwise have so few interests and pleasures outside the weary round of their household and family duties. No one who has known anything of the monotonous life of the English peasantry could do otherwise than regret that such an additional object of interest should be lost to them.

Irish Laces

Attempts have been made at various times, both during this century and the last, to assist the peasantry of Ireland by instruction in lace-making, and considerable success has often been the result. As early as 1743 the Royal Dublin Society granted prizes to be awarded by Lady Arabella Denny to those who excelled in the work; but at her death, thirty years afterwards, the undertaking came to an end. The experiment was again repeated with more permanent results in 1820, and again in 1847, at the time of the famine. It was then that crochet-work was introduced; very good patterns of old Lace were procured, and the Irish girls soon showed great skill in copying them. The work was vitiated by the use of cotton instead of linen thread, a mistake so generally made in recent Lace revivals. Cotton may look fairly well when first worked, but it does not keep its firmness and colour as does pure flax, and when washed becomes loose and woolly in appearance.

Following crochet came a better style of work, encouraged and stimulated by the "Ladies' Industrial Society," namely, Needle-point copies of old Venetian Lace. These were sometimes executed with a fair amount of skill, though, for economical reasons doubtless, the

Illustration XLIII.

Carrickmacross.

copies fell far short of the originals in the fineness and closeness of the stitches; where ten stitches were put into the old work, five or even less were made to answer the purpose in the new.

However, the Exhibition of Irish Lace at the Mansion House in 1883 did much to make it known to the purchasing public. It also encouraged those who supervised and taught the work in Ireland to raise their standard of excellence in the matter of workmanship and design, and to extend the sphere of their labours.

But it is not intended here to give any detailed account of Lace made in convents and schools, avowedly reproductions of old Italian originals, excellent though they often are. There are, however, two sorts of work, now carried on in Ireland, to which attention may be drawn as possessing some individuality, namely, the net embroideries of Limerick and the appliqué and cut cambric work of Carrickmacross. They should both be more correctly described as embroidery than as Lace in the usual sense of the word; but as they have the appearance of Lace, and are often very excellent both in effect and design, they would seem deserving of some notice. That known by the name of Limerick Lace was first made in Nottingham at the time of the invention of machine-net. The manufacture was transferred to Ireland in the year 1829 by Mr. Charles Walker, who, while studying for Holy Orders, married the daughter of a lace manufacturer, and either moved by philanthropy or as a speculation, took over to Ireland twenty-four girls to teach the work, and settled them at Limerick. It is in reality of French origin, being the same as the "Broderies de Luneville" which have been produced in France since 1800.

It is worked in two ways, either by embroidering the pattern with a darning stitch on the net, as shown in the little heading to this chapter, or with tambour stitch; spaces left in the pattern are filled in with ornamental "à jours" also worked on the net.

Carrickmacross is either appliquéd on net or cut out with a ground of "brides;" either way it is worked on muslin. The pattern is traced with close sewing, and the muslin is then cut away outside the outline. (See Illustration XLIII.)

Machine-Made Lace

In enumerating the various kinds of Lace made in Great Britain, it would not be fair to omit all mention of the productions of the Nottingham looms. It is true that as imitation Lace they are considered to rank very low in the scale of Art; but in point of execution and as marvellous triumphs of mechanical ingenuity, they surely invite admiration. If we wonder at the work of the skilful hands of the Venice and Brussels lace-makers, it may, from certain points of view, be a matter of even greater wonder that human intelligence should have compelled steam and machinery to do so nearly the same. So nearly, yet not quite.

The lace-making machine was evolved in Nottingham out of the stocking-loom; and it will be readily understood that the difficulty was not so much to make the "toilé" for the pattern—the stocking stitch was at first used as an equivalent for that—as to modify the machinery so as to divide the threads and produce the open net-work. The first idea of this invention is attributed to a common factory hand, Hammond Lindley, who, one day about the year 1760, looking at the Pillow lace on his wife's cap, conceived a plan by which he could copy it on his loom. Improvements worked out by different inventors succeeded each other, till at last, in 1810, a fairly good net was produced. It was called "Point net," and in connection with it a considerable industry sprang up in Nottinghamshire and the surrounding district. Thousands of women were employed in embroidering on this net, both by darning and tambour work. It is the work referred to already in the section on Irish Lace, as now known by the name of Limerick Lace. In the beginning of this century this Art seems to have been practised not only in Nottinghamshire but in many other parts of England, for the writer has lately seen a net scarf so embroidered, the work of an old lady upwards of eighty, still alive, who says that she made it when a child in the village school at Woolhampton in Berkshire, where the work was taught as part of the school education of the day.

But to return to Nottingham. By the time of our gracious Queen's accession, not only net, but also very good imitations of Flemish Lace had been achieved, and the extremely effective machine Lace of all kinds since produced is well known.

If it should now be asked by what signs such imitations can be detected, the answer to this inquiry must be, to a certain extent, a negative one. Machine lace is *not* made with looped stitches like Needlepoint lace, nor do we find in it the effect of plaited threads as in Pillow lace, and where neither of these easily recognised features can be discovered, the piece of Lace under examination may fairly be presumed to be imitation. As positive indications it may be observed that the "toilé" of Machine lace is often found to be ribbed, like the ribbed texture of a knitted stocking; also that whereas old Needle and Pillow lace is always worked with linen thread, Machine lace is very generally made of cotton.

It would be hopeless to attempt to describe the various substitutes for the hand-made lace-stitches which the machine-lace maker has invented; they are legion, for what he cannot achieve in one way he does in another. Nevertheless, needle-lace imitations were generally till lately very easy of detection. But where man intends to succeed difficulties seldom prove insuperable. Invention this time has come from Switzerland, and in connection with the well-known Swiss industry of embroidery on cambric and muslin. One José Heilmann, a native of St. Gall, pondering on the work of his wife's needle, thought to himself that if spinning, weaving, and printing were done by machinery, then why not embroidery? He made his wife teach him to embroider, and in six months' time he had invented a machine that worked with six needles at once. His first thought was to take it to England; but there, though his invention had many admirers, it did not find a purchaser. It was in 1838, at a time when England was so far in advance of the Continental nations of Europe in machinery, that the great heads of the manufacturing firms thought they could afford to despise foreign ideas.

Heilmann returned home, and a Swiss shopkeeper, Mange, bought his machine. It was rapidly perfected, and by 1868 hundreds of machines were turning out most excellent work.

This has recently been applied to the imitation of Venetian Point lace, with the result that a nearer approach than ever before has been made to the reproduction both of the needle-worked "toilé" and also of the "bride" work.

Yet, when so much is conceded, there remains the indubitable fact that the productions of machinery can never possess the charm of the real hand-made work. Musicians tell us that the performance of a piano-organ, even the most perfected of its kind, is flat and uninteresting as compared with the music produced by a fairly good performer. Even so with Lace made by machinery; the most perfect must by reason of its very perfection lack the impression of life which the very faults and irregularities of human handiwork can alone produce. We are so made that the imperfect even, pleases us more than the perfect, if it tells us that human beings have expended time and zeal in their efforts after perfection.

Old English Bobbins and a Lace Token.

A Summary

As a summary of what has been written in the foregoing chapters, the following few simple statements may be found useful:—

1. Lace worked out of linen, though originating in Italy, was also worked with no great variation of style in Spain, France, and England, and in the Greek islands; the designs are usually geometrical.

2. The words "Point lace," properly used, signify Needle lace only, and are misused when applied to any Pillow lace whatever.

3. The earliest Point lace was made with "brides." It was chiefly made in Venice. Some was produced at Alençon for a short time during the latter half of the seventeenth century in imitation of Venetian Point, and some may have been made in Spain.

4. Point lace with "brides" was not made in Flanders.

5. Point lace with a "réseau" ground was invented and chiefly made at Alençon. The style was adopted, both in Brussels and Venice, towards the close of the eighteenth century. Brussels Needle lace is most frequently grounded with a Pillow "réseau."

6. The most marked distinction between Point and Pillow lace is that in the former the solid parts are seen to be made of looped button-hole stitches, while that of the latter resembles woven cambric or cloth in texture.

7. Pillow lace divides itself into two classes, according to the method of its construction.

(A) When the pattern is worked by itself on the pillow and the "réseau" ground is worked in afterwards to fit round it. To this class belong "Punto di Milano," Brussels Pillow lace, and Honiton Lace.

(B) When the Lace is made all in one piece on the pillow, the same threads forming both "toilé" and "réseau" alike. To this class belong the Italian peasant Laces, all French Pillow lace, all Flemish Pillow lace, except Brussels, and all English Lace except Honiton.

8. Pillow lace made with "brides" is earlier in point of date than that made with a "réseau" ground.

9. Various Pillow laces are to be distinguished from each other chiefly by the construction of their "réseau."

10. Machine-made Lace was invented towards the end of the last century, and was not perfected till the beginning of this century. Any Lace, therefore, known to be older than 1800 must be either Point or Pillow lace.

Barbara Uttmann, A. D. 1561

Lace: Its Origin and History

Samuel L. Goldenberg

(1904)

"I have here only a nosegay of culled flowers, and have brought nothing of my own but the thread that ties them together."—*Montaigne*.

The task of the author of this work has not been an attempt to brush the dust of ages from the early history of lace in the hope of contributing to the world's store of knowledge on the subject. His purpose, rather, has been to present to those whose relation to lace is primarily a commercial one a compendium that may, perchance, in times of doubt, serve as a practical guide.

Though this plan has been adhered to as closely as possible, the history of lace is so interwoven with life's comedies and tragedies, extending back over five centuries, that there must be, here and there in the following pages, a reminiscent tinge of this association.

Lace is, in fact, so indelibly associated with the chalets perched high on mountain tops, with little cottages in the valleys of the Appenines and Pyrenees, with sequestered convents in provincial France, with the raiment of men and women whose names loom large in the history of the world, and the futile as well as the successful efforts of inventors to relieve tired eyes and weary fingers, that, no matter how one attempts to treat the subject, it must be colored now and again with the hues of many peoples of many periods.

The author, in avowing his purpose to give this work a practical cast, does not wish to be understood as minimizing the importance of any of the standard works compiled by those whose years of study and research among ancient volumes and musty manuscripts in many tongues have been a labor of love. Rather would he pay the meed of tribute to those who have preserved to posterity the facts bearing upon the early history of lace, which have been garnered with such great care.

Nevertheless, most of these works, necessarily voluminous and replete with detail, are more for the connoisseur or dilettante than for the busy man of affairs upon whom the practical aspect of lace, quite dissociated from the romance in which it is steeped, always forces itself.

It is for men of this type, and with no little misgiving, and a full appreciation of how far short of his ideal the volume must be, that the author has undertaken the compilation of this work.

Samuel L. Goldenberg

Real Flemish Point.

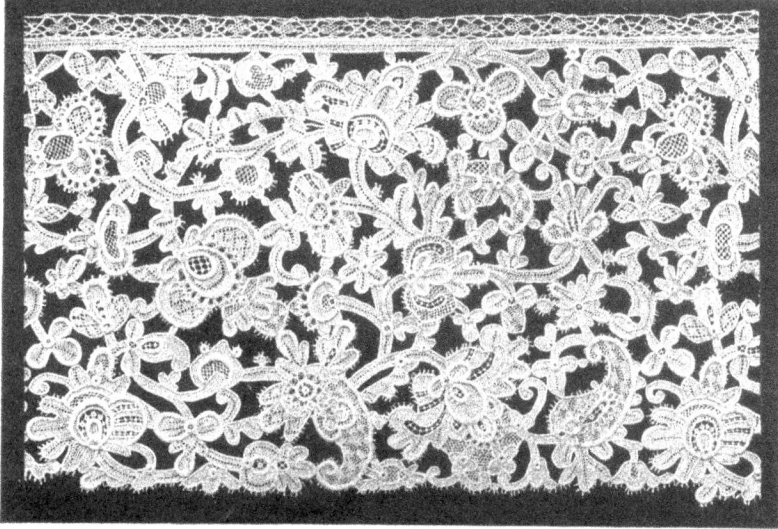

Real Point de Venise.

When, where and how lace had its origin no one will pretend to say. There is a general agreement, however, that lace, as the term is understood to-day, is a comparatively modern product, it being impossible to identify any of the antique specimens preserved from the ravages of time as belonging to a period further back than the early part of the sixteenth century.

True it is that there are specimens of woven fabrics of a lacelike character which were undoubtedly made at an earlier date, but most of the authorities who have delved deep into the subject are of opinion that lace probably does not antedate A. D. 1500.

A perusal of the available records in many tongues fails to make clear just where lace was first made. Spain, Italy, Belgium, France and Germany have all claimed the honor, and each has been able to present a great deal of testimony in support of its contention; but the records of early times are so meagre and indefinite that it is impossible to bestow the coveted honor for the discovery of the art upon any one nation.

The instrument that is responsible for lace is the needle, but the earliest forms of lace were not the woven fabric that we know to-day, but rather cutwork, which, as far as we have any authentic records, was first practiced by the nuns in the convents of central and southern Europe. This work was sometimes characterized as nun's work, and was designed almost exclusively for altar decorations and the robes of prelates, thought it was also regarded as the insignia of rank and station. Some of the specimens of this work, still preserved in museums, show that the early workers possessed a skill in the art never excelled. Of course, with the progress of time, designs have become more ornate and intricate, but many of the old patterns still survive, and doubtless will continue to survive, till the end of recorded time.

The desire to elaborate the edges of plain fabrics, whether of linen or heavier material, was an entirely natural impulse to get away from the harsh simplicity of the times. To this desire must be ascribed the beginning of the mammoth lace industry of to-day.

One authority says that coeval with these styles of decoration was drawnwork, in which the weft and warp threads of plain linen were drawn out, thus forming a square of network made secure by a stitch at each intersection. The design was afterward embroidered, frequently with colors.

Perhaps, all things considered, the lace industry received its greatest impetus during the period known in history as the Renaissance, when Europe, emerging from the severe and formal garb of the Medieval Age, began to bedeck itself in the most graceful and beautiful manner.

A number of methods were employed in the production of the lace of that brilliant period, the simplest of which consisted of forming the design independently of the foundation. Threads spreading at even distances from a common center served as a framework for others which were united in squares, triangles, rosettes and other figures worked over with the buttonhole stitch, forming in some portions openwork, in others solid embroidery. This was, in fact, the first needle-made lace, and doubtless its origin is due to the Venetians.

Through constant practice the art was developed to a very high state by the nuns, who taught their methods to the pupils of the convents, through whom the knowledge passed to the peasantry, and thus became an important industry. Perhaps, however, the development of the lace industry at this period was due more to the spread of the methods by which it was done—through books more than in any other manner—for it must be remembered that contemporaneously with the development of the industry the art of printing was in its first bloom.

As one traces the growth of lacemaking from the earliest times he is impressed with the sharp advance made at the beginning of the seventeenth century, when laceworkers, having practically exhausted the designs possible by the then known methods, invented passementerie, which were known as passements. These, speaking broadly, much resemble the passementerie of to-day.

They were made of stout linen thread in imitation of high relief work of the needle point, a thick thread being introduced to mark the salient points of the pattern. Thus the term guipure was applied to the thread lace with guipure reliefs, and the designation has since remained to all laces without grounds, in which the patterns are united by brides.

In the beginning lace was made by two entirely distinct processes, in commenting upon which we can do no better than to quote the words of Cole, which are particularly lucid and concise. He says: "It is remarkable that lacemaking should have sprung up or been invented at about the same period of time by two entirely distinct processes without relationship or evolution between them, and that the people of the countries wherein either of the inventions was made were not only unknown to each other, but apparently neither had any knowledge of the processes of lacemaking employed in the other country."

One of these processes is the employment of the needle and the single thread, wherein the work was perfected mesh by mesh, each mesh being completed as the work progressed.

The other process was by the use of many threads at once, each one attached to bobbins, for the purpose only of separating them, the meshes being made by twisting the threads a greater or less number of times. When each mesh is only partially completed the thread is carried on to the next, and so on, from side to side, the entire width of the fabric.

Felkin, in his history of embroidery and lace, says that when pillow lace was invented—about the middle of the sixteenth century—the various kinds of point lace then in use had reached a high state of perfection. Some early writers after much laborious investigation assert that pillow lace was first made in Flanders. In later years it has been almost universally attributed to Barbara, wife of Christopher Uttman; she was then dwelling with her husband at the Castle of St. Annaburg, Belgium, 1561. From the castle, where she taught the peasantry as in a school, it soon spread over the country, and women and girls of the district, finding that the making of lace was more profitable than their former employment of embroidering veils according to the Italian practice, adopted the Uttman method. No trace of this mode of making lace (by use of pillow and bobbins) can be found before this date; hence the presumption that these were the time and place of the invention of bobbin lace. Barbara Uttman died in 1575. That she was the true inventress is recorded on her tomb.

It will be seen from the foregoing that one process had its origin in Italy, and the other its origin in Belgium, though, if we accept Felkin's statement, we must accord to Italy the first honor, for he says distinctly that the Belgian peasantry gave up making lace according to the Italian method to adopt the process invented by Barbara Uttman; consequently, the Italian method must have been first. The present writer disclaims any intention to dispose of this moot question, and is only led to the above observation by reason of the high standing which Felkin's work has attained.

There are two broad divisions of lace—namely, hand-made lace and machine-made lace. In the world of commerce to-day the latter-named product, which is but a child of the former, is vastly the more important. This for the reason that hand-made lace, which is produced with such arduous toil, skill and patience, is beyond the purse of the million, and is and ever must be considered as one of the luxuries.

True, some of the simpler forms of hand-made lace are produced with relatively great facility, and the price is correspondingly cheap, as compared with the delicate, finely wrought designs, that it sometimes takes years to produce. Nor is this the sole reason for the popularity of machine-made laces, for to such perfection has the mechanical art of lacemaking attained that it is practically impossible, even for experts, to detect the difference between lace made by the deft, cunning fingers of lady or maid from the lace made possible by modern machinery.

In hand-made lace the two principal classes are the needle-point and bobbin, or pillow-made, lace. Needle-point lace is worked upon loose threads laid upon a previously drawn pattern, but which have no point of contact with one another and no coherency until the needlework binds them together. This work is done with a needle and single thread. As we have said, the pattern is first drawn, usually upon parchment; a piece of heavy linen is stitched to the parchment for the purpose of holding it straight; then threads to the number of two, three, four, or more, are laid along the many lines of the pattern, and sewed lightly down through parchment and linen. The entire figure is then carried out, both solid filling and openwork, with fine stitching, the button-hole stitch being most generally employed.

Bobbin, or pillow-made, lace is the highest artistic development of twisted and plaited threads. It is made from a large number of threads attached by means of pins to an oval-shaped cushion or pillow, each thread being wound upon a small bobbin. The design, as in the making of needle-point lace, is first drawn on stiff paper or parchment, and carefully stretched over the pillow. Then the pattern is pricked out along the outline of the drawing and small pins are introduced at close intervals, around which the threads work to form the various meshes and openings. From right to left the thread is bound lightly upon the bobbins and tied at the top of each in a loop that permits it gradually to slip off the bobbin when gently pulled, as occurs generally when working.

The worker begins by interlacing the bobbins, which are used in pairs, placing small pins in all perforations, and crossing the bobbins after the insertion of each pin. Around these pins the design is formed, the threads being crossed and recrossed and passed under and over each other with remarkable rapidity and accuracy. When the whole width of the large piece of lace is carried on together the number of bobbins and pins is very great and the work highly expensive, but it is customary to work each sprig separately, these being joined together in the form of a strip afterward by means of a curious loop-stitch, made by a hook called a needle-pin.

Scarcely had lace been invented before it had assumed almost priceless value, and it is worth while remarking here that though centuries have since elapsed, the value of these delicate, hand-wrought fabrics has not in any sense diminished. Throughout the sixteenth, seventeenth, eighteenth

Real Duchesse and Point Gaze.

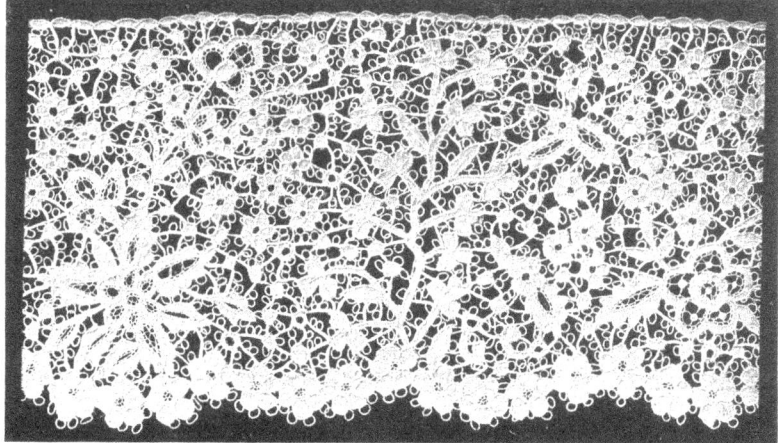

Real Carrick-ma-Cross.

and nineteenth centuries rare lace of beautiful pattern has been highly prized, some of the earliest specimens, in the possession of world-famous libraries and museums, being of relatively fabulous wealth.

By very reason of the conditions inevitably associated with its making, lace must always remain one of the dearest articles of commerce, for there is certainly nothing more rare or costly than these fine, dainty, yet withal, substantial tissues.

Perhaps of all her compeers Venice attained the highest proficiency in the production of beautiful lace. There, as we have remarked, needle-point had its origin, and many of the beautiful patterns produced by the women of the "Queen of the Adriatic" are even to-day the admiration of all who have a true appreciation of the artistic.

Venice guarded the secret of her methods with jealous care, and it was many years before the world was made familiar with the manner in which the exquisite floral designs, with their wealth of minor adornments, were worked out. Thus Italy was able to lay tribute upon the entire civilized world, and her coffers were enriched to overflowing from the receipts of the sales of lace to eastern, central and northern Europe.

Apropos of Italy's claim to the invention of needle-point, it has been claimed that the Italians originally derived the art of fine needlework from the Greek refugees in Italy, while another author asserts that the Italians are indebted to the Saracens of Sicily for their knowledge. All these claims, however, are merely speculative. For instance, no one disputes that embroidery antedates lace, and yet we have authors who endeavor to show that embroidery had its origin in Arabia, deducing from this that lace, also, must have had its birth in one of the Oriental countries. But it is a well-established fact that while we have absolute knowledge of the existence of embroidery in the countries of the Levant, there is absolutely no indication, of even the slightest value, that points to the existence of lace before it was made by the Italians and Belgians.

In the municipal archives of Ferrara, dated 1469, is an allusion to lace, but there is a document of the Sforza family, dated in 1493, in which the word "trina" constantly occurs, together with "bone" and "bobbin" lace.

Spain was, as far as the records testify, the earliest and most adept pupil of Italy in the art of lacemaking, though, as in Italy, at the beginning the work was confined in the Iberian peninsula to the inmates of the convents. Spain, too, achieved high distinction in this field, its Point d'Espagne being one of the most celebrated of all the ancient laces, even vying with the finest Venetian point. In those days, as will be recalled, the power of the Church was absolute, and the use of laces for daily wear was prohibited, though on Sundays and holidays it was greatly in evidence in the attire of those of high station.

One of the most interesting facts concerning the development of lace has to do with the patterns produced in the various localities of Europe. In the beginning the number of designs was necessarily limited, but as the industry developed and spread, and as the workers became more expert and artistic, there was an uncontrollable impulse to break away from conventional designs and to evolve new patterns. Then, too, there was something of the spirit of pride behind this movement—a sort of local patriotism, if it may so be termed. The Belgian, the Spaniard and the Frenchman were not content slavishly to imitate Italian designs, and, anxious to win a name for themselves, set about to produce new effects that would immediately identify them with the place of their origin.

Real Irish Point.

Real Valenciennes.

Thus it was, too, that various cities and towns in Italy, France, Belgium, Spain and elsewhere sought to establish for themselves an individual product of great excellence that would give to the city or town prestige and renown in the then few commercial marts of the world. This explains the various names which were given to distinct types of laces hundreds of years ago, and which designations still obtain, as, for instance, Alençon, Valenciennes, Chantilly, Honiton, Arras, Bayeux, Genoa, Florence, etc.

Another fact worthy of record is that of all the almost numberless designs that have been given to the world since the birth of lace there have been some one or two characteristics that tell as plainly as though expressed in words that each one of these designs was made at some particular period of history. It is well that this is so, for it has enabled the historian to trace, with more or less certainty, the development of the industry. In other words, a lace expert is enabled to tell from the fabric not only in what country it was made, but in what part of that country, and also the approximate date.

In the self-sufficiency of the present age we are apt to regard with a sort of supercilious disdain any story reflecting upon the supremacy of our forebears in any of the arts or the sciences; but that we cannot make, in a commercial way, such lace as was woven in the sixteenth and seventeenth centuries is beyond question. In the first place, time is lacking, and if it must be confessed, the great skill that comes only through years of constant practice is also lacking.

Modern real lace is artistic, even superior, but compared with such few specimens as have come down to us of the work of the lacemakers of old, its deficiency, particularly in the matter of the fineness of the execution and thread, is at once apparent. Hand-made lace is to-day produced all over the world; commercially its production is confined to France, Belgium, Germany, Spain, Italy and England, where large quantities are still produced. France, however, with that fostering care which she has bestowed upon her many other arts, and with that keen appreciation of the beautiful that is so inherent in her people, is far in the van in the matter of producing hand-made lace, though in respect to two or three types Belgium is in the front rank.

Coming down to the question of machine-made lace, it is necessary to observe at the outset that the same distinctions that exist between the genuine and the imitation do not obtain as applied to these fabrics. In other words, the knowledge that lace is a product of the frame rather than the fingers in no sense condemns it. For to such a high plane has the mechanical production of lace been lifted that one is almost tempted to say that the products vie in beauty of design and perfection of finish with the lace produced by hand. That there is warrant for this seeming exaggeration is borne out by the fact that not infrequently it is impossible for experts to tell the difference between two specimens of lace of the same design, one made by hand and the other by machine.

What inventors have accomplished in this respect is truly marvelous. In the beginning their efforts were not at all satisfactory, and the history of machine-made lace abounds with pathetic instances of men who sought in vain to duplicate with fidelity, by means of mechanical devices of hundreds of types and patterns, the dextrous touch of the human hand.

W. Felkin, in his history of lace manufacture, says that lace net was first made by machinery in 1768. Other authorities place the date as between 1758 and 1760. In 1809 bobbin net was invented, and in 1837 the Jacquard system was applied to the bobbinet machine.

Real Honiton.

Real Florentine.

Mrs. B. Palliser, in "The History of Lace," says of the invention of machinery for the production of lace that the credit is usually assigned to Hammond, a stocking framework knitter of Nottingham, who, examining one day the broad lace on his wife's cap, thought he could apply his machine to the production of a similar article. His attempt so far succeeded that, by means of the stocking frame invented in the previous century, he produced, in 1768, not lace, but a kind of knitting of running loops or stitches.

In 1777 Else and Harvey introduced at Nottingham the pin or point net machine, so named because made on sharp pins or points. Point net was followed by various other stitches of a lacelike character, but despite the progress made, all efforts at producing a solid net were futile. It was still nothing more than knitting, a single thread passing from one end of the frame to the other, and if a thread broke the work was unraveled. This was overcome in a measure by gumming the threads, giving the fabric a solidity and body not possible without resorting to some artificial method of this sort.

The great problem inspired the efforts of numberless inventors, and many attempts were made to combine the mechanism used respectively by the knitter and the weaver, and after many failures a machine was produced which made Mechlin net.

There are few histories bearing upon the invention of labor-saving devices that are so replete with the records of failure as is the history of the attempt to produce a practical lace machine. John Heathcoat, of Leicestershire, England, was the inventor of the machine for making bobbin net. His patents were taken out in 1809, and to him must be accorded the credit of solving for the first time the problem that had vexed the minds of so many inventors and had depleted the purses of so many capitalists.

The bobbin net machine, so named because the threads are wound upon bobbins, first produced a net about an inch in width, afterward, however, producing it a yard wide.

It was the application of the celebrated Jacquard attachment to the lace machine that has made possible the duplication of practically every pattern of lace made by hand. The machine of Heathcoat was vastly improved by John Leavers, also of Nottingham, and the types produced by him are still in use throughout England and France, though, of course, there are in these days a large number of different types of machines bearing different names, but the principle of the Leavers machine, more or less modified, obtains in practically all of the devices. Therefore a description of the process of lacemaking by the Leavers frame will serve as a description for all.

The number of threads brought into operation in this machine is regulated by the pattern to be produced. The threads are of two sorts, warp and bobbin threads. Upward of 9,000 are sometimes used, sixty pieces of lace being made at once, each piece requiring 148 threads (100 warps and 48 bobbin threads). The supply of warp threads is held upon reels, the bobbins carrying their own supply. The warp threads are stretched perpendicularly and about wide enough apart to admit a silver quarter passing edgeways between them. The bobbins are flattened in shape so as to pass conveniently between the warps. Each bobbin can contain about 120 yards of thread. By most ingenious mechanism varying degrees of tension can be imparted to warp and bobbin threads as required. The bobbins, as they pass like pendulums between the warp threads, are made to oscillate, and through this oscillation the threads twist themselves or become twisted with the warp threads, as required by the pattern that is being produced. As the twisting takes place, combs

Real Point Appliqué.

compress the twistings, making them more compact. If the bobbin threads be made tight and the warp threads slack, the latter will be twisted upon the former; but if the warps are brought to a tension and the bobbin threads be slack, then the latter will be twisted on the warps. The combs are so regulated that they come clear away from the threads as soon as they have pressed them together, and fall into position ready to perform their pressing operations again. The contrivances for giving each thread a particular tension and movement at a certain time are connected with an adaptation of the Jacquard system of pierced cards. The lace machine is highly complicated, much of its complexity being due to the mechanism by which the oscillating or lateral movements are produced. Expert workmen prepare the working drawings for the lace machine, and also perform the more important duties in its operation, but a large part of the work is carried on by women and girls.

One of the most interesting developments of the lace industry has been the gradual evolution from the work of the hand toilers to the utilization of complex machinery. In addition to the Leavers machine, which is referred to elsewhere *in extenso*, the embroidery machine plays a very important part in the making of laces. From 1870 to 1880, various efforts had been made to produce lace on the embroidery machine, and it was during this decade that the first success was achieved in the making of Oriental or net laces in Plauen. This was the first actual production of lace from the embroidering machine, and this sort of lace, which still exists to-day, is really an embroidery on a net, although usually designated as lace. A few years later a discovery was made which effected a great change in the making of laces on the embroidery machine. This was the principle of embroidering on a material which was afterward removed by a chemical process. The first article produced was called Guipure de Genes, and was at that time patented, but the patent was held to be invalid, and a few years afterward this article was generally produced both in St. Gall, where it first appeared, and in Plauen. By this method of manufacture are produced to-day all of the imitation guipure laces, such as Point de Venise, Rose Point, Point de Genes, etc.

The embroidering machine in use at the present day is constructed entirely of iron, measuring from 15 to 20 feet long, 9 feet high, 9 feet wide and weighs about 3,800 pounds. It can be operated by hand or by power. The method of embroidering is exceedingly simple. The cloth, usually somewhat over 4½ yards long, is tightly stretched in an upright position in the center of the machine, each end of the suspended strip being held firmly by means of stout hooks. The needles (from 150 to 300 in number, according to the sort of work to be done) are arranged horizontally in a framework in a straight, level row, all pointing toward the cloth and extending from end to end of same. The needles are supplied with threads about one yard in length, which are fastened by means of a peculiar knot to the eye, the latter being in the middle of the needle instead of at the end. In producing any given stitch in the pattern to be worked, the long row of needles all move forward at once at the will of the operator, and thus duplicate the stitch in every pattern or "section" along the entire 4½ yards of cloth suspended in the machine. As may be readily understood, the machine in this manner completes 4½ yards of embroidery in the same time it would take a woman with a needle to finish a single pattern. When one row is completed the strip of cloth is raised and another row is made, and so on until it is necessary to put in another length of cambric. This machine is capable of making patterns from the very narrow up to the full width of the cloth. What is known as the Schiffli, or power machine, is very similar to the hand-embroidering device, being an improvement on the latter and worked with a shuttle in addition to the needles. Its capacity is nearly eight times greater, or from 15,000 to 18,000 stitches per day, against 2,000 to 3,000 on the hand machine. To offset this advantage, however, the Schiffli machine is much more expensive, and is of delicate and complicated construction, easily got out of order and costly to repair. Until a comparatively recent date the Schiffli was not considered as a competitor of the hand machine, its work being inferior in quality and confined to simple patterns. At present, however, it is generally conceded that the goods produced by it not only compete with the hand-machine products, but are already superseding the latter to some extent. It is predicted that the Schiffli machine, operated by power, will ultimately supply all the embroidery in the low and medium grades.

The variety and adaptability of the designs which both of these machines are capable of producing are endless, and at the same time comparatively inexpensive. It is this latter fact which accounts for the great advantage of the embroidering machine over the lace machine. The preparing and setting of a design for a lace machine is very expensive, and the great cost compels the manufacturer of machine lace to turn out large quantities of one set pattern in order to get a return from his investment.

About the beginning of the nineteenth century, lace machines were first introduced into France from Nottingham, at Boulogne-sur-mer, where the industry remained for a few years and then

Real Chantilly.

Real Spanish.

moved to Calais. There this industry has developed and increased to such proportions that Calais is now the principal city for the production of fine laces of all kinds, and practically leads Nottingham in creating novelties and new and original effects. Shortly after the Franco-Prussian war the industry found a foothold in Caudry, in the north of France, where it has also developed to quite large proportions, and shares to-day a large part of the trade which has resulted from the founding of the parent industry in Calais. The kind of lace produced in Caudry is generally of a cheaper character than that produced in Calais.

In Lyons, too, there has been established for many years the industry of making laces and nettings by mechanical processes. This is still a very large industry, and about twenty years ago there was a large trade done with America in the manufacture of laces in vogue at that time, which were the imitation of the real Spanish, called "Blonde Grenade." There are still made in Lyons to-day various imitations of fine laces, which in a general way are of a different quality to the laces made at Calais or Caudry, and Lyons enjoys a reputation in regard to the character of the laces it produces which is unique in the trade.

About the year 1890, a Frenchman invented a machine similar in principle to the knitting machine, which reproduces with absolute fidelity the work of the bobbins in making pillow laces. Through this invention he was able to imitate such hand-made laces as Torchons, Medicis, etc., so exactly that experts could not detect the difference. In fact, it is the general testimony of men associated with laces for years, that the work of this machine in a great many of its aspects is one of the most important contributions of the mechanical arts in the production of lace.

Through the importation of foreign machines and foreign workmen, various attempts have been made in the United States to establish the manufacture of lace. At the present writing it is impossible to state with any definiteness what the result will be, as the experiment has been of only a few years' duration, and in the very nature of things is at this date of a tentative character.

In order that the reader may be able to distinguish the various types of hand and machine made laces, we append herewith a glossary, defining as concisely as possible the characteristics that indicate not only the manifold makes of laces, but what may be called the various subdivisions. These definitions are set forth, the writer hopes, in terms that will enable the reader to understand what each one of the various names means, both as applied commercially and descriptively.

Real Point Gaze.

Imitation Duchesse.

Characteristics of the Different Types of Lace

ALENÇON.—A fine, needle-point lace, so called from Alençon, a French city, in which its manufacture was first begun. It is the only French lace not made upon the pillow, the work being done entirely by hand, with a fine needle, upon a parchment pattern in small pieces. The pieces are afterward united by invisible seams. There are usually twelve processes, including the design employed in the production of a piece of this kind of lace, and each of these processes is executed by a special workwoman; but in 1855, at Bayeux, in France, a departure was made from the old custom of assigning a special branch of the work to each lacemaker, and the fabric was made through all its processes by one worker.

The design is engraved upon a copper plate and then printed off upon pieces of green parchment of a specified length. After the pattern is pricked upon the parchment, which is stitched to a piece of coarse linen folded double, the pattern is then formed in outline by guiding two flat threads along the edge by the thumb of the left hand, and, in order to fix it, minute stitches are made with another thread and needle through the holes of the parchment. After the outline is finished it is given to another worker to make the ground, which is chiefly of two kinds: bride, consisting of uniting threads which serve to join together the flowers of the lace, and réseau, which is worked backward and forward from the footing to the picot. There was also another ground called Argentella, consisting of buttonhole-stitched skeleton hexagons.

In making the flowers of Alençon point, the workwoman, using a needle and fine thread, makes the buttonhole-stitch from left to right, and, when she has reached the end of the flower, throws back the thread from the point of departure and works again from left to right along the thread. As a result, the work is characterized by a closeness, firmness and evenness not equaled in any other point lace.

When the work is completed the threads which bind lace, linen and parchment together are carefully cut, and the difficult task of uniting the pieces together remains to be done. This is accomplished by means of what is called the "assemblage" stitch, instead of the "point de raccroc," where the pieces are united by a fresh row of stitches.

Another way of uniting the pieces, which is used at Alençon, is by a seam which follows as far as possible the outlines of the pattern so as to be invisible. A steel instrument, called a picot, is then passed into each flower so as to give it a more finished appearance.

Alençon point is of a durability which no other lace can rival. A peculiarity in its manufacture is, that it is the only lace in which horsehair is inserted along the edge to give increased strength to the cordonnet, a practice originating in the necessity of making the point stand up when the tall headdresses formerly worn by women were exposed to the wind.

Real Duchesse.

Real Irish Crochet.

Formerly Alençon point, notwithstanding its beauty of construction, could not vie with Brussels lace as regards the excellence of floral design, but this inferiority has now been removed by the production of exquisite copies of natural flowers, mingled with grasses and ferns. Alençon point is now made not only at the seat of its original manufacture, but at Bayeux, at Burano, near Venice, and at Brussels.

Bayeux can boast of one of the finest examples of this lace ever made. It was exhibited in 1867, and consisted of a dress of two flounces, in which the pattern, flowers and foliage were most harmoniously wrought and relieved by shaded tints, which give to the lace the relief of a picture. The price of the dress was $17,000, and it took forty women seven years to finish it.

The city of Alençon had on exhibition at Paris, in 1899, a piece of lace of exquisite description, that had taken 16,500 working days to complete.

ALLOVER.—Lace of any kind which is eighteen inches or more in width, and used for yokes, flouncings and entire costumes.

ANTIQUE.—A pillow lace, hand-made from heavy linen thread, and characterized by an exceedingly open, coarse, square mesh. It is mainly used for curtains, bed sets and draperies.

ANTWERP.—A pillow lace made at Antwerp, resembling early Alençon, and whose chief characteristic is the representation of a pot or vase of flowers with which it is always decorated.

The pot or vase varies much in size and details. It is usually grounded with a coarse "Fond Champ."

APPLICATION.—A lace made by sewing flowers or sprigs, which may be either needle-point or bobbin-made, upon a bobbin-lace ground. One variety of Brussels lace affords the best example of Application.

APPLIQUÉ.—The same as Application lace.

ARGENTAN.—A needle-point lace, usually considered indistinguishable from Alençon, but which is different in some respects, its marked peculiarity being that the réseau ground is not made of single threads only, but the sides of each mesh are worked over with the buttonhole stitch. Argentan is often distinguished from Alençon lace by a larger and more striking pattern, and in some instances it is especially known by its hexagonally arranged brides. It is called after Argentan, a town near Alençon, and the lace was made there under the same direction.

ARRAS.—A white pillow lace, so called from Arras, in France, the city of its original manufacture. It is simple and almost uniform in design, very strong and firm to the touch, and comparatively cheap in price. It is made on a lisle ground. The older and finer patterns of Arras lace reached their climax of excellence during the first Empire, between 1804 and 1812, but since then they have gone out of fashion.

AURILLAC.—A pillow or bobbin lace, made at Aurillac, in France. In the early period of its manufacture it was a close-woven fabric, resembling the guipure of Genoa and Flanders, but later it resembled English point. The laces of Aurillac ended with the Revolution.

AUVERGNE.—A pillow lace made at the French city of Auvergne and the surrounding district.

AVE MARIA.—A narrow lace used for edging. (See Dieppe lace.)

BABY.—A narrow lace used for edging, and made principally in the English counties of Bedfordshire, Buckinghamshire and Northamptonshire. These laces are ordinarily of simple design and specially employed in adorning infants' caps. Though this fashion went out in Great

Real Irish Appliqué.

Imitation Point de Venise.

Britain, the ladies of America held to the trimmed infants' caps until the breaking out of the Civil War, and up to that date large quantities of this lace were exported to America.

BASKET.—A lace so woven or plaited as to resemble basket-work. It is mentioned in inventories of 1580.

BAYEUX.—There are two descriptions of lace known by this name: (a) A modern pillow lace, made at Bayeux, in Normandy, particularly the variety made in imitation of Rose point; (b) A black silk lace, popular because made in unusually large pieces, as for shawls, fichus, etc.

BISETTE.—A narrow, coarse-thread pillow lace of three qualities, formerly made in the suburbs of Paris by the peasant women, principally for their own use. The name is now used to signify narrow bordering lace of small value.

BOBBIN.—Lace made on a pillow, stuffed so as to form a cushion, without the use of a needle. A stiff piece of parchment is fixed on the pillow, and after holes are pricked through the parchment so as to form the pattern small pins are stuck through these holes into the pillow. The threads with which the lace is formed are wound upon bobbins—small, round pieces of wood about the size of a pencil, having round their upper ends a deep groove, so formed as to reduce the bobbin to a thin neck, on which the thread is wound, a separate bobbin being used for each thread. The ground of the lace is formed by the twisting and crossing of these threads. The pattern or figure, technically called "gimp," is made by interweaving a thread much thicker than that forming the groundwork, according to the design pricked out on the parchment. This manner of using the pillow in lacemaking has remained practically the same during more than three centuries.

BLONDE.—A lace so-called because, being made from raw silk, it was "fair," not white in color. Blonde lace has a "réseau" of the Lille type, made of fine twisted silk, the "toilé" being worked entirely with a broad, flat strand, producing a very attractive glistening effect. It was made at Chantilly, in France. At the Revolution the demand for this fabric ceased, as lacemakers were commonly looked upon as royal protégés. During the First Empire, however, blonde became fashionable again, and since that time the popularity of black silk blonde for Spanish mantillas alone has kept the trade in a flourishing condition. The manufacture is not confined to any one town, but is carried on throughout the province of Calvados, in Normandy, and is also made in Spain.

BOBBINET.—A variety of Application lace, in which the pattern is applied upon a ground of bobbinet or tulle.

BONE POINT.—A lace without a regular mesh ground.

BORDER.—Lace made in long, narrow pieces, with a footing on one side, the other edge being ordinarily Van Dyked or purled. During the larger part of the seventeenth century a constant supply of this lace was made at Genoa. It was commonly called "Collar" lace, from the use to which it was put. In the pictures of Rubens and Van Dyke it is frequently represented as trimming the broad falling linen collars, both of men and elderly women. It can be distinguished from Flemish lace, also employed in the same way, by its greater boldness of design. Younger women also made use of it as trimming for the shoulders of their décolleté dresses, and also for sleeves, aprons, etc.

BRIDE.—Lace whose ground is wholly composed of brides or bars, without a réseau or net.

Imitation Marquise.

Real Point d'Angleterre.

BRUSSELS.—A celebrated lace, made at and near Brussels, in Belgium; more particularly, a fine variety of the lace made there whose pattern, as compared with Alençon, has less relief, and whose fine net ground is without "picots," the knots or thorns which often decorate "brides," and also the edge of the pattern. Brussels lace, whose history is one of the most interesting in the progress of this industry, is now often regarded as an application lace, by reason of the fact that the laceworkers of that city, after machine-made net had been perfected by an English invention in 1810, adopted the plan of appliquéing their pillow-made patterns on that material. Lace so appliquéd can be recognized as distinct from that made with the "vrai réseau," or true network ground, by the fact that the net ground, though sometimes removed, is often seen to pass behind the lace pattern, and also by the character of the network. Machine-made net is composed of diamond-shaped meshes, and is made with two threads only, tightly twisted and crossed, not plaited, at their junction, and is quite unlike the Brussels pillow "réseau." Other peculiarities by which Brussels lace may be recognized are: (a) It is not made in one piece on the pillow, but the pattern is first made by itself, and the "réseau" ground is worked in around it afterward, (b) The "réseau" ground, when magnified under a glass, has a mesh of hexagonal form, of which two sides are made of four threads plaited four times, and four sides of two threads twisted twice, (c) Brussels pillow lace has two sorts of "toilé," or substance of the pattern as contrasted with the groundwork; one, the usual woven texture, resembling that of a piece of cambric; the other, a more open arrangement of open threads, having very much the appearance of the Fond Champ "réseau." It remains to be said, in spite of the fact that the above-mentioned characteristics may always be distinguished, that the Brussels pillow lace of the present day differs materially from the earlier forms, having gone through many changes and style in pattern and make. Among these are Point d'Angleterre, called such for mistaken reasons only, as it is not point lace nor made in England; and Duchesse, a name of comparatively recent date, though the style itself is of earlier origin, and was called "Guipure façon Angleterre." As regards Brussels needle-point, the earliest made closely resembles that of Alençon, though not quite so close and firm. There were also other differences, both the "cordonnet" and the "réseau" being unlike those of Alençon. From the beginning of the nineteenth century Brussels needle-point underwent changes analogous to those of pillow lace; it became Point Appliqué, in which the needle-lace pattern, instead of having a true net ground, was appliquéd on the machine-made net. But in recent years it has been noted that a return to the character of the earlier and more beautiful Brussels needle-point is being sought, the chief evidence of it being the exquisite Point Gaze, made entirely with the needle and grounded with its own "réseau."

BUCKINGHAM.—A lace originally made in the county of Buckingham, England, and of two kinds: (a) Buckingham trolley lace, whose pattern is outlined with a thicker thread, or a flat, narrow border, made up of several such threads. The ground is usually a double ground, showing hexagonal and triangular meshes; (b) A lace with a point ground, with the pattern outlined with thicker threads, these threads being weighted by bobbins larger and heavier than the rest. In general character and design these laces strongly resemble those manufactured at Lille.

CADIZ.—A variety of needle-point Brussels lace.

CARNIVAL.—A variety of reticella lace made in Italy, Spain and France during the sixteenth century.

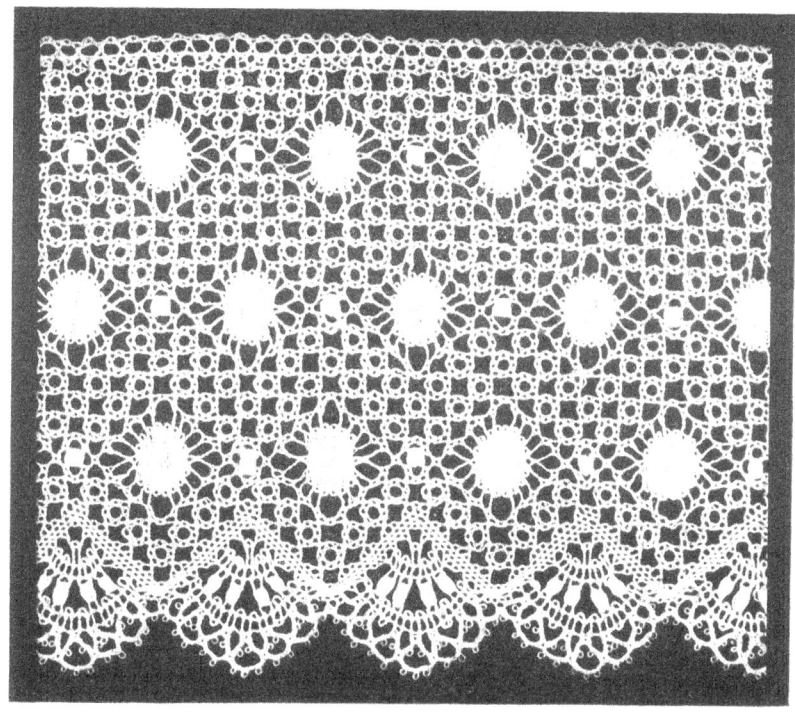

Real Torchon.

Imitation Valenciennes.

CARTISANE.—Guipure or passement, made with cartisane, which is vellum or parchment in thin strips or small rolls, covered with silk, gold thread or similar material.

CHAIN.—A lace of the seventeenth century, consisting of a braid or passement so worked as to resemble chain links. It was made of colored silk, and also of gold and silver thread.

CHANTILLY.—One of the blonde laces, of the sort recognizable by their Alençon réseau ground and the flowers in light or openwork instead of solid. It is made both in white and black silk. Black Chantilly lace has always been made of silk, but a grenadine, not a lustrous silk. The pattern is outlined with a cordonnet of a flat, untwisted silk strand. During the seventeenth century the Duchesse of Longueville established the manufacture of silk lace at Chantilly and its neighborhood, and as Paris was near and the demand of royalty for this lace increased it became very popular. At the time of the Revolution the prosperity of the industry was ruined, and many of the lacemakers were sent to the guillotine. During the ascendancy of the first Napoleon, the manufacture of Chantilly again became flourishing. Since then the industry has been driven away from that town on account of the higher labor costs resulting from the nearness of Chantilly to Paris, and the lacemakers, unable to meet this increased cost, retired to Gisors, where half a century ago there were between 8,000 and 10,000 lacemakers. The supremacy of lacemaking formerly enjoyed by Chantilly has now been transferred to Calvados, Caen, Bayeux and Grammont. The widely-known Chantilly shawls are made at Bayeux, and also at Grammont.

CHENILLE.—A French lace, made in the eighteenth century, so called because the patterns were outlined with fine white chenille. The ground was made of silk in honeycomb réseau, and the patterns were geometrical and filled with thick stitches.

CLUNY.—A kind of net lace with a square net background in which the stitch is darned. It is so called from the famous museum of antiquities in the Hotel Cluny, at Paris, and also because the lace was supposed to have a medieval appearance. The patterns used are generally of an antique and quaint description, mostly of birds, animals and flowers, and in the existing manufacture the old traditions are fairly well preserved. Sometimes a glazed thread is introduced in the pattern as an outline. Cluny is a plaited lace, somewhat similar to the Genoese and Maltese laces, and is made in silk, linen or cotton.

CORDOVER.—A kind of filling used in the pattern of ancient and modern point lace.

CORK.—A name formerly used for Irish lace in general, when the manufacture of Irish lace was principally confined to the neighborhood of Cork.

CRAPONNE.—A kind of stout thread guipure lace, of cheap price and inferior make, used for furniture.

CRETAN.—A name given to an old lace, ordinarily made of colored material, whether silk or linen, and sometimes embroidered with the needle after the lace was complete.

CREWEL.—A kind of edging made of crewel or worsted thread, intended as a border or binding for garments.

CROCHET.—Lace which is made with a crochet hook, or whose pattern is so made and then appliquéd on a bobbin or machine-made net. It is similar to needle-point lace, although not equal in fineness to the best examples of the latter.

CROWN.—A lace whose pattern was worked on a succession of crowns, sometimes intermixed with acorns and roses. It was made first in the reign of Queen Elizabeth. A relic of this lace may still be found in the "faux galon," sold for the decoration of fancy dresses and theatrical purposes.

DALECARLIAN.—Lace made for their own use by the peasants of Dalecarlia, a province of Sweden. Its patterns are ancient and traditional. It is a coarse guipure lace, made of unbleached thread.

DAMASCENE.—An imitation of Honiton lace, made by joining lace sprigs and lace braid with corded bars. It differs from modern point lace in that it has real Honiton sprigs, and is without needlework fillings.

DARNED LACK.—A general name for lace upon a net ground, upon which the pattern is appliquéd in needlework. The different laces of this kind are described under Filet Brodé, Guipure d'Art and Spiderwork.

DEVONSHIRE.—Lace made in Devonshire, England, and more frequently designated as Honiton. (See Honiton.) Formerly practically the whole female population of Devonshire were employed in lacemaking, and during the sixteenth and seventeenth centuries Belgian, French and Spanish laces were imitated in that country most successfully, as were also Venetian and Spanish needle-point, Maltese, Greek and Genoese laces. During the last century this variety in lacemaking has died out in Devonshire, and now only Honiton is made.

DIAMOND.—A lace made with a stitch either worked as open or close diamonds, and used in modern point and in ancient needle-points.

DIEPPE.—A fine point lace made at Dieppe, in France, resembling Valenciennes, and made with three threads instead of four. There were several kinds of lace made at Dieppe in the seventeenth and eighteenth centuries, including Brussels, Mechlin, Point de Paris and Valenciennes, but the true Dieppe point was eventually restricted to two kinds, the narrow being called the Ave Maria and Poussin, the wider and double grounded, the Dentelle à la Vierge. Dieppe and Havre were formerly the two great lace centers of Normandy, manufacturing in those cities having antedated that at Alençon, but the prosperity of the lace industry in both these cities was nearly destroyed at the Revolution, and though for a time encouraged under the restored Bourbons, and patronized by Napoleon III, machine-made laces have practically driven the old Dieppe point out of the market.

DRESDEN POINT.—A fine drawn lace, embroidered with the needle and made in Dresden during the latter part of the seventeenth and the whole of the eighteenth century. It was an imitation of an Italian point lace, in which a piece of linen was converted into lace by some of its threads being drawn away, some retained to form a pattern, and others worked together to form square meshes. The manufacture of Dresden point declined, and now laces of many kinds are made there, notably an imitation of old Brussels.

DUCHESSE.—A fine pillow lace, a variety originally made in Belgium resembling Honiton guipure lace in design and workmanship, but worked with a finer thread and containing a greater amount of raised or relief work. The leaves, flowers and sprays formed are larger and of bolder design. The stitches and manner of working in Honiton and Duchesse are alike.

DUNKIRK.—A pillow lace made with a flat thread, and whose manufacture was carried on in the districts around Dunkirk, a French seaport, in the seventeenth century. The best known kind was an imitation of Mechlin lace.

DUTCH.—A coarse, strong lace, made with a thick ground, and of plain and heavy design. It is a kind of cheap Valenciennes. Dutch lace is inferior in design and workmanship to those of France and Belgium.

ENGLISH POINT.—(a) A fine pillow lace made in the eighteenth century, generally considered to be of Flemish origin and manufacture, and mistakenly called "Point d'Angleterre," as it was neither point lace nor made in England. Some writers, however, assert its English origin. Owing to the protection formerly given by law to English laces, large quantities of Belgium laces are believed to have been smuggled into England under the name of "Point d'Angleterre," so as to evade the customs duties, (b) At the present day the finest quality of Brussels lace, in which needle-point sprigs are applied to Brussels bobbin-ground. (See Application lace, also Point d'Angleterre.)

ESCURIAL.—A modern silk lace, made in imitation of Rose point. The patterns are outlined with a lustrous thread or cord.

FAYAL.—A delicately made and costly lace, hand-made by the women of the Island of Fayal, one of the Azores, off the western Spanish coast. The thread used in making this lace is spun from the fiber of the leaves of the alol, a plant resembling somewhat the century plant. Great skill is necessary in the manufacture, which is restricted to a comparatively few women of the island, who have been trained to this work from childhood. The lace is marketed in France, chiefly in Paris, at a very high price, and it is very difficult for outside purchasers to buy it at any cost. The patterns are extremely elegant and original in design. Notwithstanding the delicacy of this fabric, it is remarkably durable.

FEDORA.—See Point Appliqué.

FALSE VALENCIENNES—(a) Lace resembling Valenciennes in surface and in pattern, but without the true Valenciennes net ground. (b) A term for Valenciennes lace made in Belgium.

FLAT POINT.—Lace made without any raised-work or work in relief from raised points.

FLEMISH POINT.—A needle-point guipure lace made in Flanders.

FOOTING.—A narrow lace which is used to keep the stitches of the ground firm and to sew the lace to the garment upon which it is to be worn. Sometimes the footing is worked with the rest of the design. It is used also in making lace handkerchiefs and for quilling effects.

GENOA.—A name originally given to the gold and silver laces for which Genoa was famed in the sixteenth and seventeenth centuries, but now applied to lace made from the fiber of the aloe plant, and also to Macramé lace.

GOLD.—Lace made of warp threads or cords of silk, or silk and cotton combined, with thin gold or silver gilt bands passing around it. It was anciently made of gold or silver gilt wire. It is now used chiefly to decorate uniforms, liveries and some church costumes, and occasionally for millinery. The metal is drawn through a wire, and, after being flattened between steel rollers, several strands of the flattened wire are passed around the silk simultaneously by means of a complex machine having a wheel and iron bobbins. The history of gold lace is interesting, as illustrating the oldest form of the lacemaker's art. From the days of Egypt and Rome down to medieval Venice, Italy and Spain, gold and silver gilt wire were used in making this kind of lace. The Jews in Spain were accomplished workers in this art, and in Sweden and Russia gold lace was the first lace made. In France gold lacemaking was a prosperous manufacture at Aurrillac

Real Mechlin.

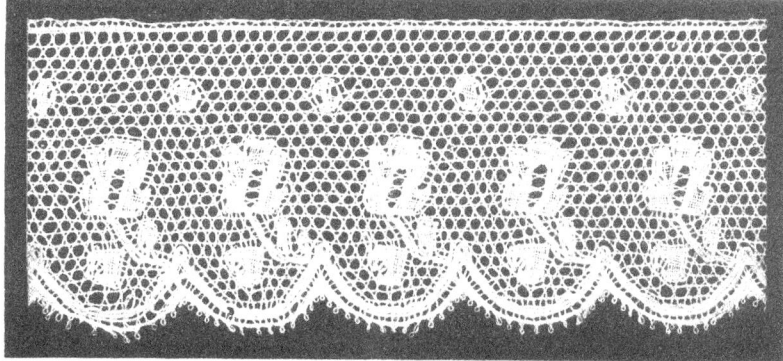

Real Point de Paris.

and Arras, at which latter place it flourished up to the end of the eighteenth century. Gold lace was imported into England at an early date, and King James I established a monopoly in it. Its importation was prohibited by Queen Anne, on account of the extravagant uses of ornamentation to which it was put, and it was also prohibited in the reign of George II, to correct the prevalent taste for the foreign manufactured lace. The attempt was unsuccessful, for we are told that smuggling greatly increased. It became a "war to the knife between the revenue officer and society at large, all classes combined, town ladies of high degree, with waiting-maids, and the common sailor, to avoid the obnoxious duties and cheat the government."

GRAMMONT.—Grammont lace, so called from the town of Grammont, in Belgium, where it was originally manufactured, is of two kinds: (a) A cheap, white pillow lace, (b) A black silk lace, resembling the Chantilly blondes. These laces are made for flounces and shawls, and were used both in America and Europe. As compared with Chantilly, the ground is coarser and the patterns are not so clear-cut and elegant as the real Chantilly.

GUEUSE.—A thread pillow lace made in France during the eighteenth century. The ground of this lace was réseau, and the toilé was worked with a thicker thread than the ground. It was formerly an article of extensive consumption in France, but, after the beginning of the nineteenth century, it was little used, except by the poorer classes. It was formerly called "Beggars' lace."

GUIPURE.—It was originally a kind of lace or passement made of cartisane and twisted silk. The name was afterward applied to heavy lace made with thin wires whipped around the silk, and with cotton thread. The word guipure is no longer commonly used to denote such work as this, but has become a term of variable designation, and it is so extensively applied that it is difficult to give a limit to its meaning. It may be used to define a lace where the flowers are either joined by brides, or large coarse stitches, or lace that has no ground. The modern Honiton and Maltese are guipures, and so is Venetian point. But as the word has also been applied to large, flowing pattern laces, worked with coarse net grounds, it is impossible to lay down any hard and fast rule about it.

HENRIQUES.—A fine stitch or point, used both in early and modern needle-point work.

HOLLIE POINT.—A needle-point lace said to have been originally called holy point, on account of its uses. It was popular in the middle ages for church decoration, but was adapted to different purposes in the seventeenth and eighteenth centuries, and various makes of lace have since been called by this name.

HONITON.—A pillow lace originally made at Honiton, Devonshire, England, and celebrated for the beauty of its figures and sprigs. The manufacture is still carried on at that town, where there is a lace school, but a similar lace is made in the leading Continental centers of the industry.

(a) Honiton Application is made by working the pattern parts on the lace pillow and securing them to a net ground, separately made. At present it is customary to use machine-made net upon which handmade sprays are sewn.

(b) Honiton guipure, which in common acceptation passes as Honiton lace, is distinguished by its large flower patterns upon a very open ground, the sprays being united by brides or bars.

Honiton braid is a narrow, machine-made fabric, the variety in most general use being composed of a series of oval-shaped figures united by narrow bars. It is of different widths, in linen, cotton and silk, and is much used in the manufacture of handkerchiefs, collars, and some varieties of lace.

Real Arabian.

Machine Irish Crochet.

The history of Honiton lace is more than ordinarily interesting, partly by reason of the doubt as to whether it really was a lace of English invention, or brought by the Flemish workmen to England. Some writers assert the former, but the stronger probability is that the art was brought from Flanders by Protestant immigrants, who fled from persecution. Whichever theory is held, the development of the industry at Honiton, and its close resemblance to other lacemaking processes in Belgium, Holland and France, afford an excellent illustration of the interdependence of lacemakers in all countries upon each other as regards improvements resulting from new ideas. Honiton, if it was brought from Flanders originally, afterward repaid the debt by the beauty and celebrity of its designs, which served as examples for Continental lacemakers. The very attempt to protect its manufacture in England, by imposing prohibitive duties, only increased the desire to receive foreign suggestions, and to smuggle foreign laces into England, while the ingenuity of Continental manufacturers succeeded in copying the best Honiton designs, and even in improving upon them. The English lacemakers at Honiton were, however, at first unsuccessful in their attempts to rival the best laces of the Continent, especially Brussels. Although they had royal patronage, and the whims and lavish expenditure of the court of Charles II were at their service, together with protective duties, it was not until the reign of George II and George III that English lace substantially improved. This resulted from substituting the working of the true Brussels net ground, or vrai réseau, for the old guipure bar ground. The patterns were also formed of detached flower sprays, and soon the Honiton product became almost unrivaled. This superiority continued until about 1820, when machine-made net was introduced, and the old exquisite net ground, made of the finest Antwerp thread, went out of fashion by reason of the commercial demand for an inferior product. Honiton guipure is now the chief form of lace made at that town. As regards composition of the patterns of Honiton laces, as well as finish and delicacy of execution, much improvement has been manifested during the last twenty years by reason of better schools for design, and the rivalry promoted by international exhibitions.

IMITATION.—Machine-made lace of any kind. It often rivals real lace in fineness, but necessarily its mechanical regularity of pattern detracts somewhat from the artistic character of the result. Constant improvement in processes, however, has in some laces made the resemblance to the hand-made product so close that even experts can hardly recognize the difference. If it were asked how the imitation lace can be distinguished from needle-point, the answer is that it is not made with looped stitches like the latter, nor has it the effect of plaited threads, as in pillow lace. Again, the toilé of machine-made lace is often found to be ribbed, and this lace is very generally made of cotton instead of the linen thread with which old needle-point and pillow lace is made. In the invention of substitutes for hand-made lace stitches Switzerland has been the leader, and by 1868 hundreds of machines, perfected from the invention of a native of St. Gall, were turning out a close imitation of the hand-made work. The most recent triumphs of this description are the imitations of Venetian point, in which a nearer approximation than ever before has been made to the needle-worked toilé, and also of the bride work. But, notwithstanding the marvelous results attained in machine-made lace, they are the triumphs of mechanism which cannot displace the superiority, and charm, and rarity, of the finest hand-made work. In the latter the personal equation, the skill and the loving, workmanlike fidelity of the individual toiler to his task impart a quality which dead mechanism can neither create nor supersede. Machine-made lace may be predominantly the lace of commerce, but hand-made lace is the natural expression and embodiment of a delicate and difficult art, and thus it will ever remain.

INSERTION.—A kind of lace, embroidery or other trimming used to insert in a plain fabric for ornamental purposes. It is made with the edges on both sides alike, and often a plain portion of the material outside the work, so that it may be sewn on one side to the garment for which it is intended and to the plain part of the lace or border on the other.

IRISH.—A term denoting a variety of laces made in Ireland, of which the two most individual and best-known kinds are the net embroideries of Limerick and the appliqué and cut cambric work of Carrick-ma-cross. Other varieties, which are imitations of foreign laces, are Irish point, resembling Brussels lace; black and white Maltese; silver, black and white blondes. The Limerick embroideries, for they cannot be strictly called lace, are an imitation of Indian tambour work, and consist of fine embroidery in chain-stitches upon a Nottingham net. Carrick-ma-cross, or Irish guipure, is a kind of so-called Irish point lace, made at the town of that name, but which is really nothing more than a species of embroidery, from which part of the cloth is cut away, leaving a guipure ground. It is not a very durable lace. The most popular patterns are the rose and the shamrock. Irish crochet is an imitation of the needle-point laces of Spain and Venice; that is to say, it resembles these laces in general effect. There is also a needle-point lace made of rather coarse thread, and used exclusively in Ireland and England. The manufacture of laces in Ireland is carried on by the cottagers, by the nuns in the convents, and in several industrial schools founded for that purpose. It has only become a popular industry within the last twenty-five years, as the costumes of the people in earlier times did not require lace ornamentation, and there was a widespread and deep-rooted aversion to the adoption of English fashions in clothing so long as certain sumptuary laws were unrepealed.

Afterward, under slightly more liberal conditions, English fashions were gradually adopted, and with them came the demand for a cheap Irish lace, as the foreign laces were too expensive. Not until 1743 was there any official attempt to encourage the industry, but in that year the Royal Dublin Society established prizes for excellence in lacemaking. This attempt lasted until 1774. In 1820 a school was opened in Limerick for instruction in the now celebrated lace or embroidery first made in that town; but in the famine years of 1846-48 more effectual measures were taken to spread a knowledge of the art, and several schools were opened in different parts of the country. The Irish have never made a lace that can in any sense be called national, but great skill has been developed in the imitations of the foreign fabrics, and the Irish name has been so closely associated with some of them that they are popularly considered a native Irish product. The exhibition of Irish laces at the Mansion House in London in 1883 added materially to the reputation of these fabrics.

IRISH TRIMMING.—A plain-patterned, woven lace, formerly used in ornamenting muslin underwear, pillow slips and the like.

JESUIT.—A modern needle-point lace, made in Ireland, and so called on account of the tradition as to the introduction of its manufacture after the famine of 1846.

KNOTTED.—A term applied to the old Punto a Groppo, of Italian manufacture originally, and consisting of a fringe or border made of knotted threads. It is commonly called Knotting in all English-speaking countries. The modern Macramé is made like the knotted laces.

LILLE.—A lace made at Lille, in France, noted for its clear and light single réseau ground, which is sometimes ornamented with points d'esprit. It is a lace of simple design, consisting of a thick run thread, enclosing cloth-stitch for thick parts, and plaitings for open parts. The old Lille lace is always made with a stiff and formal pattern, with a thick, straight edge, and with a square instead of the usual round dots worked over the ground. Lille was distinguished as a lacemaking city as far back as 1582, and from that year until 1848 the industry was successful, but since the latter year there has been a steady decline, as more remunerative occupations have gradually drawn away the younger workers from lacemaking. The Lille pattern was similar to that of the laces made at Arras and Mirecourt, in France, and in Bedfordshire and Buckinghamshire, in England, but none of the latter could rival the famous single réseau ground.

LIMERICK.— (See Irish Lace.)

LUXEUIL.—A term applied to several varieties of hand-made lace produced at Luxeuil, France. They are stout, heavy laces, mostly made with the use of braid, and are much used for curtains and draperies.

MACRAMÉ.—A word of Arabic derivation, signifying a fringe for trimming, whether cotton, thread or silk, and now used to designate an ornamental cotton trimming, sometimes called a lace, made by leaving a long fringe of coarse thread, and interweaving the threads so as to make patterns geometrical in form. It is useful in decorating light upholstery. Macramé cord is made of fine, close-twisted cotton thread, prepared especially for the manufacture of Macramé trimming, and also for coarse netting of various kinds. The foundation of all Macramé lace or trimming is knots, made by tying short ends of thread either in horizontal or perpendicular lines, and interweaving the knots so as to form a geometrical design, as above mentioned, and sometimes raised, sometimes flat. This necessitates the forming of simple patterns. This lace is really a revival of the old Italian knotted points, which were much used three centuries ago in Spain and Italy for ecclesiastical garments. It appears in some of the paintings of the early masters, notably Paul Veronese. The art has been taught during all the nineteenth century in the schools and convents along the Riviera. It is developed in great perfection at Chiavari, and also at Genoa. Specimens of elaborate workmanship were in the Paris Exhibition of 1867.

MACKLIN.—Another name for Mechlin lace.

MALINE.—A name sometimes applied to Mechlin lace, especially to the varieties whose ground is distinguished by a diamond-shaped mesh.

MALTESE.—A heavy but attractive pillow lace, whose patterns, of arabesque or geometric design, are formed of plaiting or cloth-stitch, and are united with a purled bar ground. It is made both in white silk and thread, and also in black Barcelona silk. There is also a cotton machine-made variety, used chiefly in trimming muslin underwear. The history of Maltese lace is interesting from the fact that the kind originally made in that island by the natives, which was a coarse variety of Mechlin or Valenciennes, of an arabesque pattern, was in 1833 superseded by the manufacture of the white and black silk guipures now so widely known as Maltese lace. This improvement was due to Lady Hamilton Chichester, who brought laceworkers over from Genoa to teach their craft in the island. Some of the patterns from that time showed the influence of the Genoese instruction. Maltese lace is made not only in Malta, but in Auvergne and Lepuy in France; in Buckinghamshire and Bedfordshire, in England, and also in the Irish lace schools.

Imitation Point d'Alençon.

Ceylon and Madras lace also resembles Maltese. Formerly shawls and veils of much beauty and value were made of this lace, but the manufacture is now confined chiefly to narrow trimmings.

MECHLIN.—A pillow lace originally made at Mechlin, Belgium, and whose special characteristics are the narrow, flat thread, band or cord, which outlines the pattern, and the net ground of hexagonal mesh. Sometimes the mesh is circular. The net ground is made of two threads twisted twice on four sides and four threads plaited three times on the two other sides. In this it differs from Brussels lace, whose plait is longer and whose mesh is larger. The lace is made in one piece upon the pillow, the ground being formed with the pattern. The very finest thread is used, and a high degree of skill is necessary, so that the resulting fabric is very costly. It is a filmy, beautiful and highly transparent lace, and preserves for a very long time its distinguishing peculiarity of a shiny thread or band surrounding the outlines of the sprigs and dots of the design. The earliest Mechlin designs were very like those of Brussels lace, though not so original and graceful; but in this respect later Mechlin laces showed marked improvement. The fundamental difference between the two, however, was that Mechlin was worked in one piece upon the pillow, while the Brussels pattern was first made by itself, and the réseau or net ground was afterward worked in around it. The manufacture of Mechlin has long been on the decline, the French Revolution seriously injuring the industry; and when the trade was revived and encouraged under Napoleon, the exquisite patterns of former times had been partly forgotten or were too expensive for popular demand. At the time of its highest popularity it was called the Queen of Laces, sharing that title with the finest Alençon point. Mechlin sometimes had an ornamental net ground called Fond du Neige, and also a ground of six-pointed Fond Champ, but these kinds were rare. It has always been a very great favorite with the English, and appears in most of their family collections of laces. There was a fine collection of this lace at the Paris Exhibition of 1867 from Turnhout, Belgium, as well as from other lace manufacturing centers.

MEDICI.—A name for a variety of modern torchon lace, whose distinguishing peculiarity is the insertion effect, the lace being very like an ordinary insertion, with the exception of having one edge finished with scallops. The Medici design is also characterized by plain, close-woven work, the close work alternating in equal amount with the openwork, the contrast between them heightening the effect.

MÉLANGE.—A heavy, black silk lace, distinguished by its mingling of Spanish patterns with ordinary Chantilly effects. The edge is usually plain and straight, but is sometimes ornamented with a fine silk fringe.

MIGNONETTE.—A light pillow lace, with an open ground resembling tulle, made in narrow strips. It was one of the earliest of pillow laces, and flourished greatly during the sixteenth, seventeenth and eighteenth centuries. It was made of Lille thread, and the chief places of its manufacture were Arras, Lille and Paris, in France, and in Switzerland.

MIRECOURT.—A lace made of detached sprigs upon a net made at the same time with the pattern. In the seventeenth century it was a French guipure lace of more delicate texture and varied design than other guipures. Mirecourt, in the Department of the Vosges, and its environs, were the center of the industry. The manufacture was begun at an early date, and for centuries only hempen thread was used, the result being a coarse guipure: but during the early part of the seventeenth century a finer lace of more delicate pattern was produced, and it began to be exported in

Real Cluny.

Real Bruges.

considerable quantities. Before the union of Lorraine with France, in 1766, there was less than 800 laceworkers in Mirecourt, but in 1869 the number had increased to 25,000. During the last century the French demand for this lace increased far beyond the foreign demand, and it became desirable to produce a greater variety of pattern. This was done with great success by imitating the best designs. Another recent improvement at Mirecourt is the making of application flowers, and though these are not yet as finished as the Brussels sprigs, they bid fair to supply the French market, so as to make it to that extent independent of Belgium. The lace made at Mirecourt is mostly white. The work is similar in process and equal in quality to that of Lille and Arras.

NANDUTI.—A lace made by the natives of Paraguay, Ecuador and Peru, South America, from the soft, brilliant fiber of the agave plant. It is made in silk or thread by a needle on a cardboard pattern. In Peru and Ecuador it is also needle-made in the form of small squares and united together.

NEEDLE-POINT.—Real lace of any kind worked with a needle, on a parchment pattern, and not with bobbins or on a pillow. The distinction between needle-point and bobbin-made, or pillow lace, is also illustrated by the solid part of the pattern, and also the ground of the former. In needle-point the solid parts are invariably made of rows of buttonhole stitches, sometimes closely worked and sometimes with small open spaces left in the patterns. The "brides" in needle-point consist of one or two threads fastened across from one part of the pattern to another, and then closely buttonholed over; it will be found, also, that true needle-point is made with only one kind of stitch, the looped or buttonhole stitch already mentioned, and that this is constant amid all varieties of design in this kind of lace. Pillow lace, on the contrary, has a "toilé" made of threads crossing each other more or less at right angles; its "brides" consist of twisted or plaited threads, and the "picots" are simple loops, while the network ground of pillow lace is of far greater variety than that of needle-point. In all kinds of pillow lace the net groundwork is made by twisting and plaiting the threads, sometimes in twos and sometimes in fours. Briefly speaking, the fundamental difference between needle-point and pillow lace is that the former is made with looped stitches throughout, while the latter is made with twisted or plaited threads, which last is really weaving, though it is done with bobbins and the hand instead of with the loom.

ORIENTAL.—A lace made on the embroidering machine, which by combined needle and shuttle action produces either simple or complex designs upon netting. The action of the Schiffli machine somewhat resembles that of a sewing-machine, and the product is more properly called embroidery than lace. The openwork effects are produced either by the action of chemicals upon the foundation material, or by the use of the scissors. The threadwork results from the combined action of the shuttle and needles. St. Gall, Switzerland, and Plauen, Saxony, are the chief manufacturing centers for these laces, which include trimming and border laces, curtains, bed sets, shams, and the like. In the broad historical sense, Oriental laces and embroideries refer to the products of the East, especially to the Chinese, Indian, Japanese, Persian and Turkish. All these were remarkable for the labor expended upon them, their great cost, and the originality and boldness of idea and coloring which marked their design.

OYAH.—A guipure lace or openwork embroidery, made by means of a hook in a fashion similar to crochet. The pattern is often elaborate, and in silks of many colors, representing flowers, foliage, etc. It is sometimes in relief.

Imitation Mechlin.

Imitation Torchon.

PARCHMENT.—Lace in whose manufacture parchment has been used, whether in the pattern for the worker's guidance, or for stiffening the fabric, as in Cartisane lace. In old accounts of laces, the term was often applied to those made on the pillow to distinguish them from needle-point laces, and it was derived from the pattern on which pillow laces were worked.

PASSEMENT.—A term applied to the oldest class of pillow laces, at a time when they were of comparatively simple construction, being little more than open braids and gimps. This designation was in use until the middle of the seventeenth century. The word is now applied to a decorative edging or trimming, especially a gimp or braid. It is an old French word, and in the country of its origin included in its meaning both lace and embroideries. It has an interesting literary association, having figured, under the slightly altered form of "passemens," in a satirical poem published at Paris in 1661. The poem, which is entitled "La Révolte des Passemens," is dedicated to Mademoiselle de la Trousse, a cousin of Madame de Sévigné, and was probably composed by one of her literary friends. It is a protest against a sumptuary law passed in the previous year to check the lavish expenditure on laces imported from Venice and Italy, and is interesting as an account of the best laces of that day, among which are "Poincts de Gènes, de Raguse, de Venise, d'Angleterre et de Flanders," as well as the "Gueuse" of humbler pretensions. The various laces are supposed to revolt against the law excluding them from France, and especially from their place in the exalted society of the court. Mesdames les Broderies—

"Le Poincts, Dentelles, Passemens,
Qui par une vaine despence,
Ruinoient aujourd 'hui la France"—

call an indignation meeting. One of them hotly demands what punishment shall be meted out to the court for such treatment—

"Dites moi je vous prie
Poincts, dentelles ou broderies,
Qu'aurons nous donc fait à la cour," etc.

Various laces speak their mind freely in reply, but most of them are gloomy as to the future, while a few try to take a philosophical view of the situation, and resign themselves to an humbler though still useful fate. An English lace, "une Grande Dentelle d'Angleterre" answers

"Cet infortune sans seconde
Elle fait bien renoncer au monde
　　* * * *
Pour ne plus tourner à tout vent
Comme d'entrer dans un Convent."

The laces of Flanders are not so submissive as that, being too vain and ambitious for renunciation of the world and life in a convent, and their angry opposition starts a little tempest of debate, fierce resolution alternating with despair. A black lace in hopeless mood hires herself out with a game merchant, for nets to catch snipe and woodcock. An old gold lace, in grandmotherly style, tries to comfort the younger ones, by reminding them of the vanity of the world. She knows all about it—she, who has dwelt in king's houses. The Flanders laces cry out that rather than give in they would sooner be sewn to the bottom of a petticoat. Some of the younger ones declare they must still have amusement, having had so much, and rather than renounce the world they will seek refuge in the masquerade shops. The point laces, with the exception of Aurillac, then resolve to go each to his own country, when suddenly the humble but plucky Gueuse lace, the lace of the common people, arrives from a village near Paris and encourages the others to fight it out.

The next morning they all assemble and agree upon a plan of campaign, but before doing so take stock of their qualifications and prospects. Poinct d'Alençon has a good opinion of herself; a Flanders lace says she made two campaigns under the king, as a cravat; another had been in the wars under the great Marshal Turenne; another was torn at the siege of Dunkirk; and all had done something worth notice. "What have we to fear?" asked an English lace. A Poinct de Gènes, of rather flabby character, advises the English lace to go slow. Finally open war is declared, and the laces all assemble at the fair of St. Germain to be reviewed by General Luxe. The muster roll is called by Colonel Sotte Depense, and the various regiments and battalions march forth to victory or death. But they got neither, for at the first approach of the royal artillery they take to their heels, are captured and condemned to various punishments.

The gold and silver laces, the leaders of the rebellion, are sentenced to the fate of Jeanne D'Arc, to be burned alive; the points are condemned to be made into tinder for the sole use of the King's Musketeers; others are to be made into cordage or sent to the galleys. But pardon is obtained through the good offices of cunning little Cupid— "Le petit dieu plein de finesse," and the rebels are restored to their former position.

The poem illustrates the policy of most European governments at that time, a policy of excluding foreign manufactures of all kinds; and in the case of laces, the fear of encouraging wasteful habits among the rich, who offered a tempting opportunity for royal extortion, was too useful a pretence to be passed by. But all these efforts were fruitless to discourage the growth of lacemaking. The passion for beauty in personal adornment would not down. The engravings of Abraham Bosse, which portray the dress and manners of that time, humorously depict the despair of the fashionable lady over the prospect of giving up her laces. She is represented as attired in plain hemmed linen cuffs, collar and cap of Puritanical severity, bemoaning her sad fate, in heartbreaking strains, as she sorrowfully packs away her rich lace-trimmed costumes. Her sadness was not unduly prolonged. Colbert, the great French statesman, saw that laces would be smuggled if they were legally prohibited, that the rich would have them at any cost, so he encouraged foreign lacemakers to come to France, and the manufacture was thus promoted.

PILLOW.—Lace made on the pillow or cushion, both pattern and mesh being formed by hand. See Needle-point lace.

PLAITED.—A pillow lace of simple geometrical design, often made of strong and stiff strands, such as gold thread or fine braid. The pattern, besides being geometrical in design, is open, and has no grounds. For ordinary purposes tinsel is used instead of real gold, and the lace is then employed for theatrical purposes. Historically considered, the plaited laces made of gold, silver or silk thread, took the place of the Italian knotted laces of the sixteenth century. Those produced at Genoa and in Spain were the best, and they are made in Spain to-day, chiefly for church uses. The thread plaited laces of the seventeenth century were used to trim ruffs and falling collars, but went out of fashion when flowing wigs came in, as the latter hid the collar and would not allow ruffs to be worn. At the present time plaited laces have become known under the name of Maltese and Cluny, and are made at Auvergne, in France, Malta, and in the English counties of Bedfordshire and Buckinghamshire.

PLAUEN.—A name applied to any kind of lace made at Plauen, Saxony, or elsewhere, upon the embroidering machine, such as Oriental, tulle and chiffon lace, Point de Venise, Point d'Irlande. Plauen led in the manufacture of this kind of lace, having begun it in 1881, from which year dates the importance of that city as a lace market. The manufacture was gradually developed. Only the tulle variety of embroidery lace was produced until 1886. The distinguishing feature of this was that the hollow effects were made by opening the tulle meshes by hand. Then, in 1886, an openwork process was invented by which chemical action was employed to remove a woolen or silk foundation from the cotton-embroidered pattern, or a cotton foundation from a silk embroidery that had been worked on it. This made it possible to form the pattern by the embroidery machine in the same way as in the case of ordinary embroidery. The wool foundation, which is necessary to be removed in finishing the goods, is dissolved by the action of certain chemicals without changing the cotton or silk pattern. In this way the most difficult and complicated patterns of real lace can be imitated. Plauen manufacturers have for the most part taken the old and costly hand-made laces of former times for their models; but they have also originated new and tasteful designs from time to time.

POINT APPLIQUÉ.—Point lace whose design is separate from the net ground, to which it is afterward applied. At the present time the net ground is usually machine-made. The word "point," however, in this connection, is of variable application, sometimes signifying Point Appliqué, and sometimes denoting lace, whether pillow or needle-point; that is, worked in sprays and laid upon a machine-net ground. (See Application lace.)

POINT D'ALENÇON.—See Alençon.

POINT D'ANGLETERRE.—See English Point.

POINT DE GAZE.—A very fine, gauze-like lace, made entirely with the needle and grounded with its own net. Point de Gaze is the result of an attempt of the Brussels lacemakers to return to the best early traditions of needle-point. Point de Gaze differs, however, from the finest old needle-point in certain respects, partly necessitated by modern taste in design, and partly from the need of great economy in labor costs. For example, the execution is much more open and delicate than in the early lace of this description, but this very delicacy and slightness are made use of to produce a very elegant effect. Part of the toilé, or substance of the pattern, is made in close and part in open stitch, giving an appearance of shading, and the open parts are very tastefully ornamented with dots. The result does not in all respects equal the softness and richness of the early lace, but if Point de Gaze seems thin and loose in comparison, and if the patterns seem less ideally beautiful, nevertheless the later work has a unique lightness and delicacy to which the earlier lace did not attain. It certainly is the most etherial and delicately beautiful of all point laces. Its forms are not emphasized by a raise outline of buttonhole stitching, as in Point d'Alençon and Point d'Argentan, but are simply outlined by a thread.

Real Renaissance.

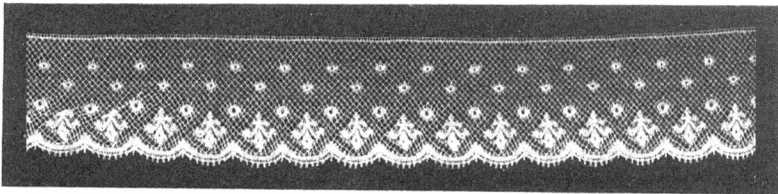

Machine Valenciennes.

Point de Gène.—A name at present applied to a species of lace made both in cotton and silk at St. Gall and Plauen, and recognized by its regular net ground and large, open patterns in heavy stitchwork. It is a popular trimming for women's dresses. Point de Gène, or Gènes, was originally one of the laces made at the city of Genoa and in the surrounding country during the seventeenth century, both the pillow and needle laces made there being deservedly famous. Gold and silver thread and gold wire were used in the manufacture of the earliest needle-point laces at Genoa, and the gold wire was drawn out in exact imitation of the early Greek method. One of the best Genoese laces resembles the early Greek points in patterns. There was also a guipure lace, made from aloe fiber, as well as the knotted lace now known as Macramé. The last named is the only lace at present made in Genoa, and along the seacoast.

Point d'Esprit.—A term applied to a small oval or square figure, peculiar to certain varieties of early guipure, and ordinarily composed of three short lengths of parchment or cord, placed side by side and covered with thread. These oval or square figures were most commonly arranged in the form of rosettes. At present the term Point d'Esprit denotes a much smaller solid or mat surface, used to diversify the net ground of some laces. It is in the form of small squares that set at close and regular intervals. In standard histories of lace the term is also used as synonymous with embroidered tulle, made in Brittany, Denmark and around Genoa.

Point d'Irlande.—A coarse, machine-made imitation of real Venetian point lace. It is popular for dress trimmings, and is manufactured in a great variety of widths in cotton and silk. It has no net ground, the patterns being united by brides.

Point de Milan.—A guipure lace with a small mesh ground, and the pattern distinguished by striking scroll designs. The flowers in the pattern of hand-made Point de Milan are flat, and have the appearance of having been wrought in close-woven linen. Milan point was made at the city of that name in 1493. Gold and silver thread were first used, but the Milan points were finer than these, and fully equal to the best Spanish and Venetian points.

Point de Paris.—Originally a narrow pillow lace, resembling Brussels. The term is now generally applied to a machine-made cotton lace of simple pattern and inferior quality. In its making a design whose figures, such as flowers and leaves, are outlined with a heavy thread, is worked upon a net ground. Point de Paris is distinguished by the net, which is hexagonal in form.

Point de Venise.—See Venice Point.

Point.—Same as Needle-point lace, made wholly by hand, with the needle and a single thread.

Pot.—Lace whose pattern is distinguished by the figure of a vase or deep dish, and sometimes by that of a basket containing flowers. It is the best-known lace made at Antwerp, and was formerly in common use in that city for decorating women's caps. The vase and basket figures vary much in size and design. Some have considered this pattern to be a survival from an earlier design, including the figure of the Virgin and the Annunciation, but this is not certain.

Powdered.—Lace whose ground is strewn with small, separate ornaments, such as flowers, sprigs, or squares, like Point d'Esprit. The term is applied also to whitened lace.

Renaissance.—A modern point lace, whose patterns are made of narrow braid, and united by bars or filling of different kinds. It is generally ornamented with circular figures and scroll-work, stitched in place by needle and thread, the intervening spaces or groundwork, being composed of a variety of fancy openwork. Irish Renaissance, Luxeuil and Battenberg are the other names for this lace.

Lace: Its Origin and History

Imitation Point de Venise Combined with Point Glaze.

Rose Point.—See Venice Point.

Saxony.—Fine-drawnwork embroidered with the needle, in much demand in the eighteenth century. At the present time the term is somewhat vague, denoting many kinds of laces made in Saxony, especially in imitation of old Brussels lace. Though the latter is the best that is made, a coarse guipure lace, known as Etervelle, and plaited lace has the greatest sale.

Seaming.—A narrow openwork insertion, gimp or braiding, with parallel sides, used for joining two breadths of linen, instead of sewing them directly the one to the other. The name is given to a similar lace used for edgings, as in the trimming of pillow-cases and sheets. During the sixteenth and seventeenth centuries this lace was very popular, though the name "seaming" was then applied to any kind of lace used for a particular purpose—namely, to insert in the linen or other fabric wherever a seam appeared, and often where no seam was really necessary. The lace first used for this purpose was cut-work; then Hollie point became fashionable, and afterward the custom grew to be so common that cheaper laces were employed. There is still in existence a sheet decorated with cut-work that once belonged to Shakespeare.

Silver.—A passement or guipure wholly or in large part composed of silver wire, or of warp threads of silk, or silk and cotton combined, wound with a thin, flat ribbon of silver. See Gold lace.

Spanish.—A general term applies to the following four different kinds of lace: (a) Needle-point lace, brought from Spanish convents after their dissolution, though the art of making it is thought by some to have been learned in Flanders, (b) Cut and drawnwork made in Spanish convents, of patterns usually confined to simple sprigs and flowers, (c) A modern black silk lace with large flower patterns, (d) A modern needle-made fabric, the pattern usually in large squares. The machine-made black and white silk laces, with their flower patterns, are from Lyons and Calais, France. Much could be said about the uncertain application of the term "Spanish" in regard to certain kinds of lace. It has often been inaccurately used. For instance, "Spanish Point" and "Point d'Espagne" have been misapplied to Italian laces, in the same way that "Point d'Angleterre" has been misapplied to Brussels lace. In the four kinds of Spanish lace above enumerated, it is noticeable that some are of Flemish origin. A lace known for certain to be of Spanish origin is a coarse pillow guipure made in white thread and also of gold and silver. It is a loosely made fabric consisting of three cordonnets, the center one being the coarsest, united by finer threads running in and out across them, and with brides to join the parts of the pattern and keep them in shape. It is well known that large quantities of lace that have the characteristics of raised Venetian Point were used in Spain, both for court dresses and church purposes, such as the ornamentation of vestments and altars. During the invasion of Napoleon the churches and monasteries were pillaged and the laces contained therein were scattered abroad and sold as being of Spanish origin, though many of them were not.

The graceful Spanish headdress, the mantilla, has been chiefly made in the province of Catalonia, out of black and white Blondes, but it is inferior to a similar lace of French manufacture. The most celebrated of the Spanish laces are the gold and silver fabrics, known as Point d'Espagne, the Blonde laces and Spanish or Rose point. The first-named is a very old lace, was known in Spain as early as the middle of the fifteenth century, and is made with gold and silver threads, upon which a pattern is embroidered in colored silk. The Blondes, which have been

Real Maltese.

Real Guipure.

already mentioned, have thick though graceful patterns upon a light net ground. Rose point is wholly made with the needle and is very like Venetian point, being considered, in fact, as a variety of the latter. The close resemblance is accounted for by the fact that this kind of lace was made by the inmates of religious houses, which were transferred from one country to another at the will of their superior and carried with them the secret of a difficult art. The Rose points, some of which are not raised, are formed with a pattern-worked net in buttonhole stitches, the parts of the pattern being joined together by brides. The raised Rose points are recognized by their thick cordonnet or outlining of the pattern.

TAMBOUR.—Lace made with needle embroidery upon a machine-made net, generally black or white Nottingham. It is chiefly made in Ireland and commonly included among the Limerick laces.

TAPE.—A lace made with the needle, except that a tape or narrow strip of linen is wrought into the work and is the distinguishing feature of the pattern. These plain or ornamented tapes or braids, arranged so as to form the pattern, have always been peculiar to this kind of lace. The patterns are connected together with either bride or net grounds. The earliest were made with a bride ground and simple cloth stitch, but gradually very elaborate designs were wrought as part of the braid-like patterns and united by open-meshed grounds. In the seventeenth and eighteenth centuries the braid and tape laces included the large majority of coarse pillow laces made in Flanders, Spain and Italy.

THREAD.—Lace made from linen thread as distinguished from silk and cotton laces. Black thread is a misnomer for Chantilly.

TORCHON.—A coarse pillow lace made of strong, soft and loosely twisted thread. In Europe it is known also as "Beggars'" lace, and the old French Gueuse lace was similar to Torchon. The patterns generally are very simple and formed with a loose stout thread and the ground is coarse net. Torchon is now also machine made.

VALENCIENNES.—A solid and durable pillow lace having the same kind of thread throughout for both ground and pattern. Both the pattern and ground are wrought together by the same hand, and as this demands much skill in the manipulation of a great many threads and bobbins, the price of Valenciennes is very high. The mesh of the ground is usually square or diamond shaped, very open and of great regularity. It is a flat lace, worked in one piece, and no different kind of thread is introduced to outline the pattern or to be wrought into any part of the fabric. This affords a ready means of distinguishing the hand-made variety of this lace. The Valenciennes now made is not so beautiful in design and construction as the fabric of an earlier date, especially in the latter part of the eighteenth century. It is usually of narrower width and is easier to learn how to make.

Valenciennes was first made at the town of that name, which, though originally Flemish, was transferred to France by treaty; and the manufacture at this town was carried on under conditions which assured the superiority of the lace produced there. The difference between the Valenciennes product and that of other towns could be detected by the softer "feel" in the former case, because the moist climate of Valenciennes gave a smoother action to the bobbins when used in manufacture; and it is interesting to note that the lace was made in underground rooms. These peculiarities earned for lace made in that town the name of Vraie Valenciennes, and it brought a higher price

Imitation Irish Crochet.

than the Valenciennes of the surrounding villages. The thread was spun from the finest flax. To buy a yard of a flounce or a pair of broad ruffles was a serious matter for the purchaser unless he was wealthy. The labor cost was high even in those days of low wages; from 300 to 1,200 bobbins were required in a piece of fine work. The history of the changes in Valenciennes patterns is, to some extent, a history of deterioration in elegance of design. The first patterns were exquisitely beautiful, the designs often being wrought in grounds that were varied in several ways even in one piece. The designs afterward became simpler, and octagon and hexagon meshes came to take the place of the close grounds of earlier manufacture. Since 1780 the lighter and less expensive laces of Lille, Brussels and Arras have partly ousted the more beautiful, costly and durable product of Valenciennes, while changes in modern dress have stopped the demand for some articles which were formerly among the fashionable mainstays of the industry; for example, men's ruffles.

The French Revolution practically destroyed lacemaking at Valenciennes, and the industry was transferred to Belgium. The lace produced there was, however, given the name of False Valenciennes. Alost, Bruges, Ypres, Ghent, Menin and Courtrai became centers of the manufacture, and the lace made in each town had a distinguishing feature in the ground. For example, the Ghent ground is square meshed, the bobbin being twisted two and one-half times. At Ypres, the ground is square meshed, but the bobbins are twisted four times. In Courtrai and Menin, the bobbins are twisted three and a half times, and in Bruges three times. As an illustration of the fact that the making of old Valenciennes is a lost art, it is interesting to note that the last important piece of work executed within that town was a headdress presented by the town to the Duchesse de Nemoms on her marriage in 1840. The headdress was made by old women, the few real Valenciennes laceworkers then surviving, with the praiseworthy and patriotic object of showing the perfection of the product of former days. There are several machine-made varieties of Valenciennes. English Valenciennes is chiefly made at Nottingham; it is also called Platt and Normandy Valenciennes. It is an imitation of the early hand-made lace, to the extent of having a similar diamond-meshed ground. Its pattern is without relief, and the threads of which it is made are no heavier than the ground. French Valenciennes is made mostly at Calais. Its pattern is usually outlined by a stouter thread than that forming the ground, and it has a finer finish and softer "feel" than the English Valenciennes; in fact, it is an excellent imitation of the real. Italian Valenciennes is a narrow, fine-threaded lace, used for trimming fine underwear.

VENICE POINT.—A needle-point lace made at Venice during the first half of the seventeenth century. It is somewhat difficult to apply the name exclusively to any one of the several varieties of Venetian point made at that time; but Venetian Raised point, whose pattern is of large, beautifully designed flowers in decided relief and united by brides or bars, is commonly called Venetian point. Other names applied to this kind of lace are Rose point, Venetian Flat point, Carnival lace, Cardinal's point, Pope's point, and Point d'Espagne. These names simply register the various changes of style and manufacture in the history of this lace. With the exception of Point d'Espagne, which has a less valid claim to be called Venetian point than the others, the various names given serve roughly to suggest the distinction between three separate stages in point of style and date of the fabric known broadly as "Punto tagliato a foliani," or Venetian point. They are generally given as follows: (1) Venetian Raised point, or Gros Point de Venise, under which is included Rose point; (2) Venetian Flat point, or Point Plat de Venise, with its later variety,

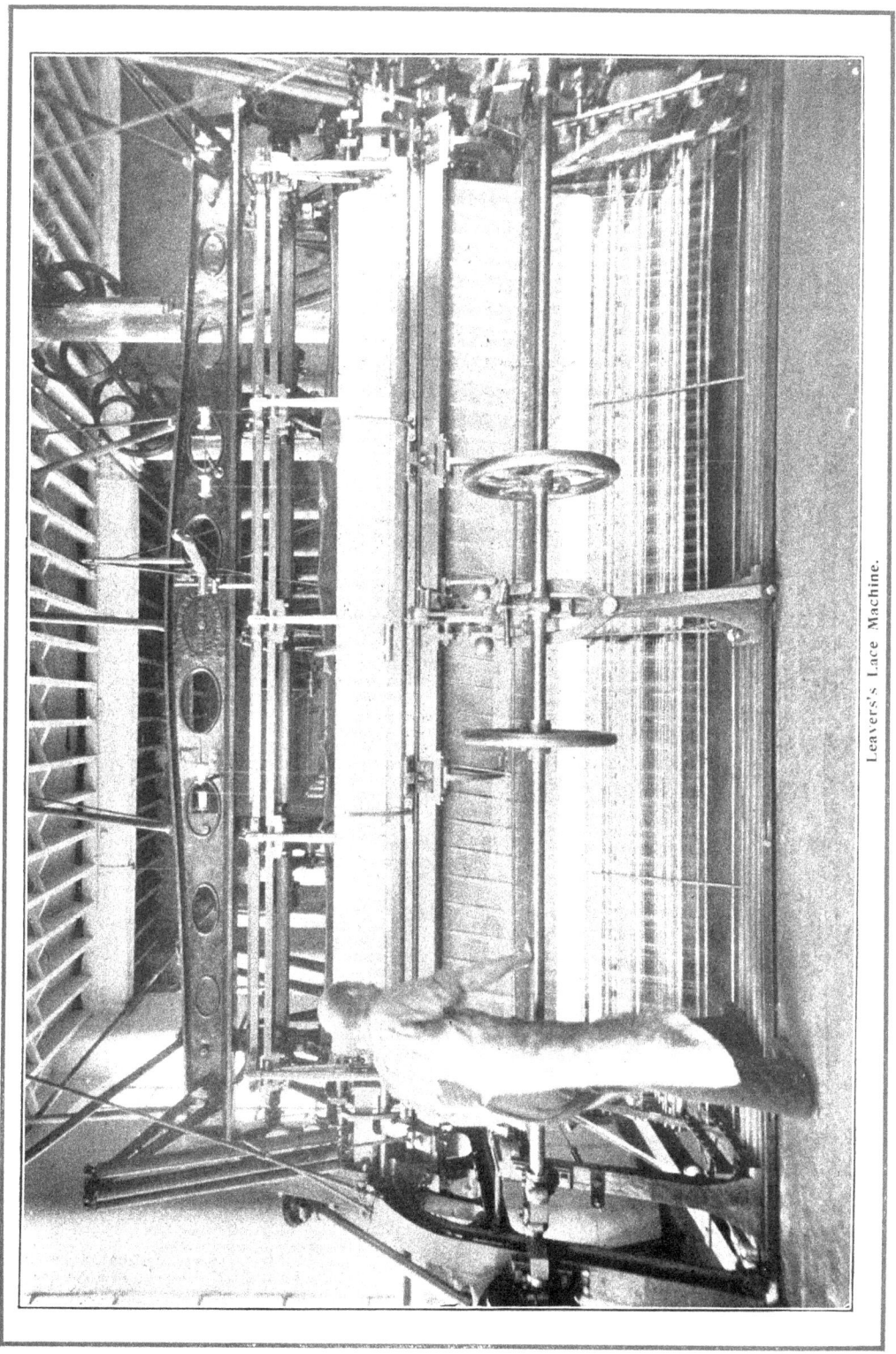

Leavers's Lace Machine.

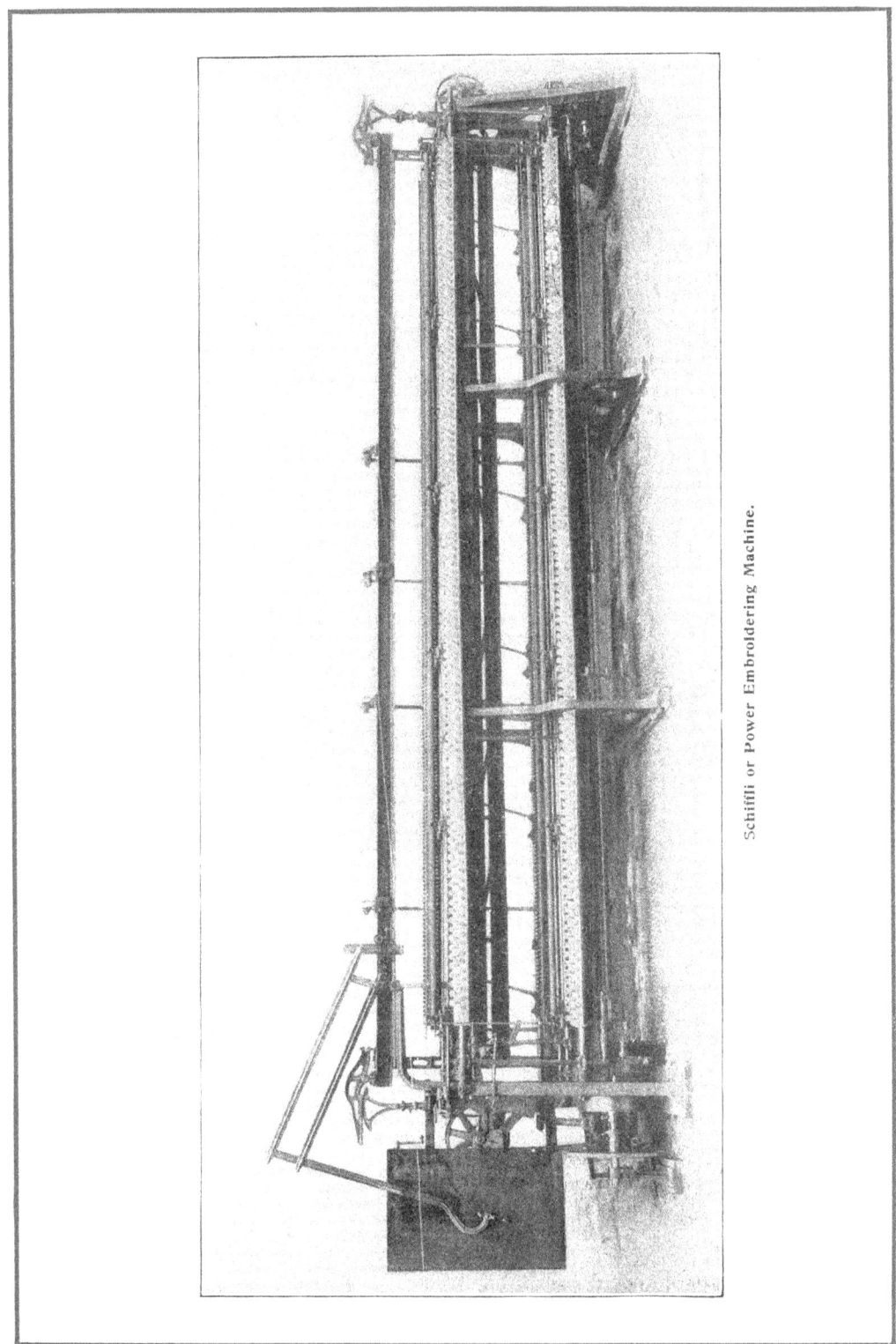

Schiffli or Power Embroidering Machine.

known as Coraline point; (3) Grounded Venetian point, or Point de Venise à Réseau, which includes Burano point, so called from the island near Venice, where it was made. With regard to Raised point, it is worth noting, in addition to the characteristics already referred to, that the flower design is of a freedom and continuity that make the pattern so filling that there is very little space left for the ground, the bridework merely serving to hold the pattern strongly together. The cordonnet, or outlining thread, is unusually prominent, and the raised part is no less remarkable for its boldness in design than for its delicate workmanship. An Italian poet has described this work as "sculptured in relief." In Raised point the skill of the laceworker was informed by the instinct for beauty in such a degree as to produce one of the highest types of the art. Rose point resembles Raised point in all essential features, the only difference being that the designs are smaller and the ornamentation more abundant. The pattern is less filling and the connecting brides more prominent.

Flat Venetian point is marked by an absence of the prominent raised work, the designs are more attenuated, and the brides are altogether more prominent than in the Raised point. Coraline point is a variety of Flat point, which must be considered a deterioration in design on account of its ill-connected and irregular pattern, which was originally supposed to imitate a branch of coral. There is no raised work, the ground meshes are ill-arranged and ill-shaped, and on the whole this lace marks the decadence of an art formerly almost perfect. It is more like an imitation of a free growth of plants, the tangled growth of a state of nature, as compared with the order and beauty of art. The grounded point, the last stage of development of Venetian lace, began to be made to supply the markets of France after the fine old Venetian point had been excluded by protective laws. The Venetian lacemakers then adopted the réseau or net ground made at Alençon. The ground is composed of double twisted threads, and has a rounder mesh than Alençon, and there is no outlining cordonnet. In this variety of Venetian point, which was produced during the latter half of the eighteenth century, the pattern is not so well arranged as in others, and there is a redundancy of ornamentation. The manufacture of Venetian point is now almost extinct. The machine-made variety, produced on the Schiffli embroidery frame, is now made at Plauen and St. Gall. (See Plauen lace.)

YAK.—A stout, coarse pillow lace, made from the fine wool of the Yak. The patterns are of simple, geometrical design, connected with plaited guipure bars that form part of the pattern, being made out of the same threads at the same time. The term is also applied to a machine-made worsted lace, produced in black, white and colors. It is used as a trimming for undergarments, shawls and petticoats.

YPRES.—A pillow lace resembling Valenciennes, but sometimes with bolder designs and rather large lozenge or square mesh in the ground; also a type of Valenciennes.

www.ingramcontent.com/pod-product-compliance
Lightning Source LLC
Chambersburg PA
CBHW041139170426
43199CB00023B/2921